Wires above South East London

Woolwich to Gravesend by
Tram and Trolleybus

Robert J Harley

Heathfield Publishing

Cover One of the locations which has changed little over the years is the crossroads outside St John's Church, High Street Eltham. Former East Ham car 81 turns west towards central London, whilst RTL 185 (KGK 849) heads in the opposite direction on route 21 to Sidcup. The bus still has its austerity restricted destination blind display. The low wooden buildings to the left of the tram were constructed by the LCC as passenger shelters and facilities for staff. At the time of writing (2020) they were all still in existence. *Alan Watkins*

© Robert J. Harley 2020

First published 2020

ISBN 978 1 85414 451 5

Published by Heathfield Publishing in Heathfield, East Sussex

Printed in the EU

CONTENTS

The Last Car from Bexleyheath

DARTFORD FROM MARTYR'S MEMORIAL.

In this view over the rooftops the clock on the Parish Church of Holy Trinity Dartford is striking the hour of 10 o'clock. Life in this Kentish market town is a world away from fashionable West End shops, opulent financial institutions of the Square Mile and the hustle and bustle of one of the world's largest trading ports. Route 96 car 1714 climbs East Hill; it is actively pursued by an open top bus. True to local dairy farming traditions, a lorry loaded with milk churns heads downhill. This is the last summer of tramway operation. This section of track out to Horns Cross will not be converted to trolleybus operation. *Richard Stevenson Collection*

Introduction and Acknowledgements

This book covers the period 1871-1959 in an area once part of the County of Kent. Successive boundary changes since 1889 have enlarged Greater London, which now includes the two boroughs of Greenwich and Bexley. Dartford and Gravesend have remained in the Garden of England.

The routes described in this volume ran on home territory for your author. A fascinating experience for a small child was enhanced by the sights and sounds of Beresford Square, Woolwich in the early 1950s with a seemingly endless procession of trams and trolleybuses, threading their way past market stalls and Saturday morning shoppers.

Others have shared this passion for electric traction. I am very grateful to those enthusiasts, past and present, without whose assistance the following chapters could not have been written. My thanks go to Geoffrey Baddeley, George Gundry, D.W.K Jones, Alan A Jackson, John Meredith, John Wills, John Price, C.Carter, John Kennett, Dave Jones, Colin Withey, John Gent, John Prentice, Ken Glazier, Mick Webber, David Willoughby and Barry Cross.

Special mentions are due to Alan and Ann Watkins, who both have contributed much to the study of public transport and local history; also to Richard Stevenson, who has supplied rare street views from his collection. Conversations with Ted Oakley, George Tapp and Richard Elliott added considerably to my knowledge of the working practices of the local tramways. I would also like to thank David Voice and Bob Appleton of the Tramway & Light Railway Society and Peter Waller of the Online Transport Archive.

Your author is very grateful to Colin Withey for sharing his expertise on the M class and associated municipal rolling stock in North Kent.

Much of the original manuscript for this book was based on research undertaken from the mid 1960s onwards. During this period I was much indebted to staff at the London Transport Archive and the local history libraries of Lewisham, Greenwich, Bexley and Dartford. I acknowledge the influence of the 1963 work entitled *Tramways of Woolwich and South East London* by 'Southeastern'. Further important reference works are listed in the Bibliography section.

Imperial measurements were in common use during the tram and trolleybus period. Where appropriate, metric equivalents have been given. Lengths in legal documents of the era are often quoted in miles and chains. A mile = 1760 yards = 1.6 km. A chain = 22 yards = 20.11 metres.

As regards traditional units of currency, a pound (£) was divided into twenty shillings; one shilling (1/-) comprised twelve pence. Common coins tendered in fares included the penny (1d), the 'thruppenny bit' (3d) and the sixpence (6d). The last was known in the vernacular as a 'tanner'.

Robert J Harley
Heathfield, March 2020

1 Penny Rides

On Saturday 4th March 1871, Greenwich was 'en fete'. Flags were unfurled; bunting adorned shops and houses. Excited bystanders lined the pavements. In the early afternoon, when the cortege came into view, the locals cheered the five decorated, horse drawn tramcars, which arrived at the new eastern terminus of the Pimlico, Peckham & Greenwich Tramways Company. Invited guests then made for the Ship Hotel in order to celebrate the occasion. No doubt they were relieved to stretch their legs after sitting on the hard wooden seats. It is recorded the ladies in the party were provided with cushions for the ride.

Public service commenced the next day. Trams ran every six minutes alternately to the foot of Westminster Bridge or to Stamford Street, Blackfriars. The future looked bright for tramway promoters. Penny fares, with a maximum of 3d to the end of the line, enticed passengers to take the tram in preference to walking or other forms of transport. Amalgamation with the Metropolitan Street Tramways Company to form the London Tramways Company would create an enterprise serving the principal traffic arteries of South London, thus generating profits for the shareholders.

At that time another favourable indication was the imminent publication of the Board of Trade (Tramways Metropolis) Report, which was to be presented to Parliament on 3rd May. The text detailed expansion plans throughout London. In the south east of the capital powers were sought for new routes to Woolwich, Blackheath, Lewisham and Catford. In light of these encouraging signs, what could possibly go wrong?

The date is 4th March 1871, at a time when photography was still in its infancy and stove pipe hats were all the rage. On first glance, the occasion of the arrival of the first horse trams in Greenwich appears to be a men only celebration. However, the ladies in the inaugural party were riding in the lower saloons of the tramcars. Note the skeletal nature of the stairways and upper deck railings on these early vehicles.

We enter the first decade of the twentieth century. An LCC crew now staffs a former WSELT vehicle. Although horsecar design did not progress much over three decades, the fitting of decency panels at least ensured that women could join the menfolk on the top deck. Passengers' headgear definitely reflected social status. A lone 'Tommy Atkins' reminds us of the importance of the military to Woolwich. This tram is working the narrow gauge shuttle from Rainton Road, Charlton to Beresford Street, Woolwich. It provided a connecting link between two sections of the standard gauge, electrified LCC system.

As often happens in the UK, readers will not be surprised to learn that political prejudice, biased reporting and vested interests combined to stymie plans to provide London with a cheap and reliable transport system. Railway companies operating suburban steam trains objected to the newcomers because they feared any competition. The horse bus people just wanted the whole of the City, West End and Westminster to themselves. They lobbied Parliament to exclude 'the rail bound menace' (their words) from fashionable streets in the centre of town. The tactic worked. Trams were obliged to terminate their journeys on the approaches to the Thames bridges. Working people from South London then had to proceed on foot the rest of the way.

In spite of these setbacks, the time was opportune to extend the Greenwich line past the folk who lived along the Woolwich Road and out as far as Plumstead. Fortunately, the locals did not share the snobbery of their West End counterparts. Behind the secure walls of the giant Woolwich Arsenal employees benefited from an extensive rail network, but when they left the confines of the site, shanks's pony was the order of the day. They needed transport to and from work.

On 28th October 1880, the Woolwich & South East London Tramways Company was formed. Parliamentary powers were obtained and track laying commenced the following April. Public service between Beresford Street, Woolwich and Plumstead, the Plume of Feathers, was inaugurated on 4th June 1881. A spur along Powis Street was also constructed, but this branch proved something of a white elephant and fell into disuse. Meanwhile, through cars on the newly constructed main line to Greenwich welcomed their first fare paying passengers on 21st November 1882.

At the Greenwich terminus in Trafalgar Road opposite the King William IV public house, Woolwich bound tramcars met vehicles belonging to the London Tramways Company. There was an interchange of passengers, but differences in track gauge prevented through services. The LTC used standard gauge tracks (4ft 8½ins/1435mm), whilst the WSELT opted for the narrower spacing between the rails of 3ft 6ins/1067mm. This disparity presented a minor inconvenience in horse tram days; however, as we shall see, it would cause significant difficulties, when the permanent way was later reconstructed for electric traction.

This very rare view illustrates a Woolwich tramway speciality, the lunch time extra. Employees at the Arsenal would receive their midday sustenance delivered by family members to the gate on Plumstead Road. Not everyone was confined to the work bench. Some skilled workers, who lived nearby, managed to take the tram home for their meal break. After all, it was better than walking. *Richard Stevenson Collection*

It is doubtful whether anyone but a hardened tram enthusiast would have made the journey all the way from central London to the end of the track by the Plume of Feathers. It was easier and quicker to take a South Eastern Railway train from Charing Cross and alight at Plumstead Station, which had opened for business on 18th July 1859. In fact most of the tramway's clientele were short distance riders. Anybody who wanted to venture further afield could take advantage of a WSELT summer excursion to Bexleyheath. A fare of 2d was charged for a place on a horse drawn brake fitted with transverse seats.

The annual return ordered by Parliament, dated 21st June 1886, contains the following figures:

Gravesend, Rosherville & Northfleet Tramways
Gauge 3ft 6 ins
Total Track Length (single and double line) 1mile 65 chains.
Gross Receipts £1,638.
Working Expenditure £1,536.
Number of Horses 10.
Number of Cars 4.

Woolwich & South East London Tramways
Gauge 3ft 6ins
Total Track Length (single and double line) 4 miles 63 chains.
Gross Receipts £12,517.
Working Expenditure £11,377.
Number of Horses 152
Number of Cars 15.

Plans there were aplenty for horse tramways as far as Dartford, calling in at Welling, Bexleyheath and Crayford along the way. None were realised. Promoters in Gravesend were more successful. As mentioned in the Annual Return, a short narrow gauge horsecar line opened for business on 15th June 1883. Although this was a very modest start, it was here in this North Kent town, situated on the banks of the River Thames, that a pioneering, revolutionary advance in transport was about to happen.

2 Kent Goes Electric

The honour of being in the vanguard of powered public transport in the UK belongs to Gravesend and Northfleet. In 1888 the recently formed Series Electric Traction Syndicate Ltd. signed an agreement with the Gravesend Tramways Company to equip a short line. Two new fangled, horseless tramcars, which appeared to move as if by magic, began public service on Monday, 29th April 1889. Passengers were carried a distance of 1000 yards/914 metres from Ye Olde Leather Bottel inn along High Street to a terminus opposite Station Road, Northfleet. Power at 200 volts DC was supplied by means of an enclosed underground conduit, situated directly beneath one of the running rails. The whole set up was in the nature of an experiment. As such, it lasted a disappointingly short time. By mid November 1890 this novel enterprise was at an end. Tracks were retained for horsecar operation, but nothing more was seen of the pair of electric trams.

Undaunted by early setbacks, technological advances continued apace, so that by 1901 the British Electric Traction Company (BET) had arrived on the scene with the intention of constructing new standard gauge lines in the town. Officials were aware there was a likelihood of schemes in Dartford and Bexley being brought to fruition. The idea of a direct line of tramway connecting to the vast London network became a distinct possibility.

An artist has captured the scene of the citizens of Northfleet, as they witness the birth of the modern age. In fact, the over size depiction of the new electrical wonder adds to the impact of the vehicle. In the distance a humble horsecar has been drawn realistically to scale. In spite of its imperfections this is still a remarkable document, which gives the reader a good idea of the fashions, buildings and street life of the late Victorian era.

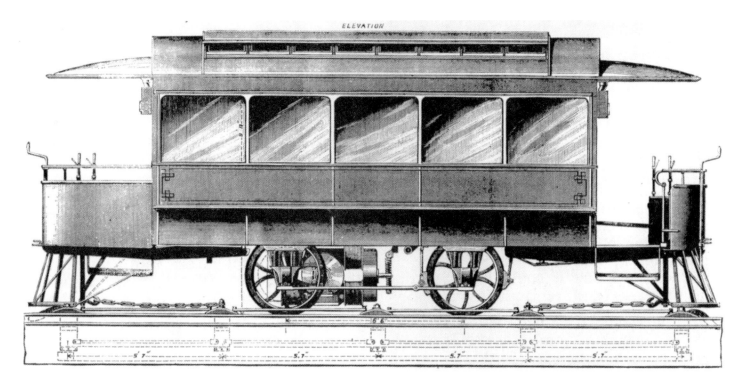

The Northfleet experiment was featured in the British technical press. Here is a side view of one of the experimental vehicles.

The local horse trams were retired on 30th June 1901, thus permitting complete reconstruction of the permanent way. The section from Leather Bottel to the Clock Tower opened on 2nd August 1902. This was followed on 22nd September by extensions to the original route as far as Swanscombe and Denton. A branch along Pelham Road also came into service on the same date. From 30th January 1903 passengers were carried on the link along Dover Road between the Leather Bottel and the Pelham Arms. Finally, on 4th December 1903, electric trams began to run along Windmill Street as far as the Old Prince of Orange public house. At the beginning of operations the fleet consisted of twenty vehicles. All were housed in a brick built depot just off the Dover Road.

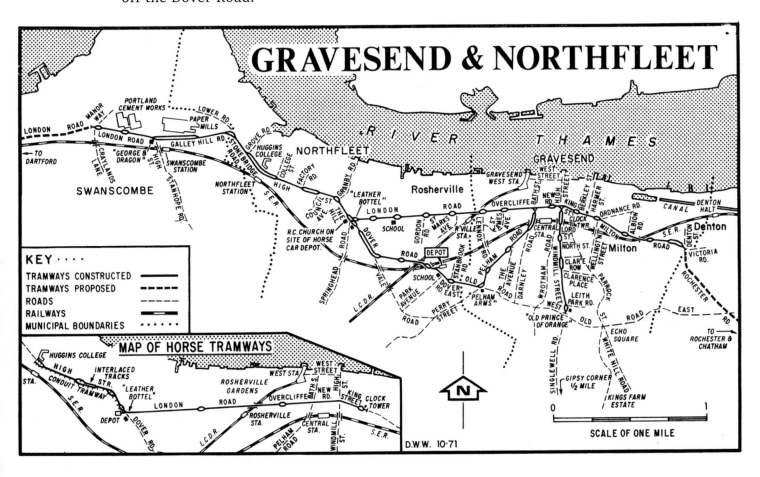

Fashionable citizens of Gravesend appreciated their new transport system, which was quicker, cleaner and more reliable than the old horsecars. The conductor is collecting fares and giving out tickets on the top deck of a passing tramcar. Meanwhile in the street below two elegant Edwardian ladies take a stroll in the sunshine. Sea faring folk were a common sight in the town; the character in front of the ladies is a dead ringer for Captain Haddock of Hergé's *Adventures of Tintin* fame. *Bob Appleton Collection*

The BET provided Gravesend with a privately run tramway, but the tide in other areas of Metropolitan Kent was flowing firmly in favour of municipal operation, which would benefit ratepayers rather than shareholders. A less attractive feature of publicly owned tramways was the rise of a degree of parochialism. Elected councillors sometimes failed to see the bigger picture, thereby hampering progress towards integrated services and through running over neighbouring networks. As we shall see, this lack of vision was to affect co-operation between operators.

Gravesend was closely followed by Bexley Urban District Council, whose line between the Plume of Feathers, Plumstead and Northumberland Heath, via Welling and Bexleyheath Broadway, opened on 1st October 1903. The track layout was principally single line and passing loops. Signals supplied by the Harrison Automatic Electric Semaphore Company ensured that no two vehicles going in opposite directions could meet between loops. The initial fleet of twelve single truck, open top cars was stabled in a depot to the south of Bexleyheath Broadway, a few yards from the end of the track at Gravel Hill.

Bexley was fortunate to have acquired the right to lay rails across the county boundary into the territory of the Metropolitan Borough of

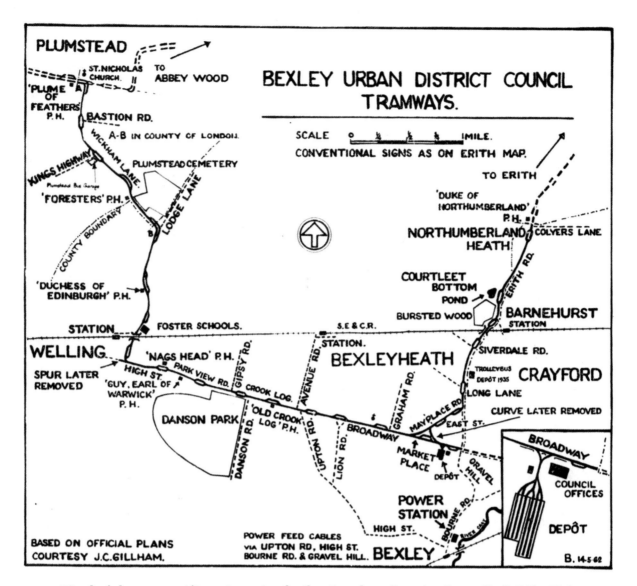

Woolwich, a constituent part of the London County Council (LCC). This short section of track guaranteed Bexley UDC an important voice when it came to negotiations with the representatives from County Hall. The LCC had inaugurated electric traction on 15th May 1903, with a view to providing new services throughout South London. The acquisition of a number of horse tramway companies would eventually include the WSELT narrow gauge line, which abutted Bexley tracks at the Plume of Feathers.

The foothold gained by Bexley was not replicated by Erith Urban District Council. The line from Northumberland Heath to Abbey Wood, opened 26th August 1905, ended at the junction with Knee Hill, right on the frontier between Kent and the County of London. Plans by Erith to reach Plumstead came to nought. They were to be frustrated by their larger neighbour.

After all this tramway activity, there was still a gap to be filled between Gravel Hill, Bexleyheath and London Road, Swanscombe. Powers were obtained by Dartford under the 1896 Light Railways Act. On 12th July 1905 construction commenced at the Bexleyheath end of the project. The main line out to Horns Cross opened on 14th February 1906, as did the two branches to the depot in Victoria Road and to Wilmington. In contrast to Bexley the council did not wish to operate the system, but agreed a lease with J.G.White & Co., which from January 1909 came under the auspices of Balfour, Beatty & Co.

Frustratingly, the Dartford rails at the end of the line were some mile and a half short of the Gravesend tracks at Swanscombe. Horns Cross was fated to remain the easternmost tram terminus of the London network.

Bexley UDC car 3 pauses in the Broadway for the official photograph. The vehicle is in near original condition, but has the rocker panels painted in dark maroon. The vehicle lacks indicator boxes and electric headlights. At the start of operation oil lamps were placed on the dash of each tram. It was thought that, if the power failed at night, the whole vehicle would not then be plunged into darkness. *Richard Stevenson Collection*

The inauguration of any British municipal tramway became an important date in the social calendar. As can be seen here, the fire brigade has posted a guard of honour around car 3 of the Dartford system. Just in front of the depot other invited guests clamber on the trams to find their seats for the opening procession. A young lady leans out very precariously from an upper floor window of an adjacent house. Nobody wanted to miss this event. All they need now are the tram crews and they can commence their tour of the town. *Richard Stevenson Collection*

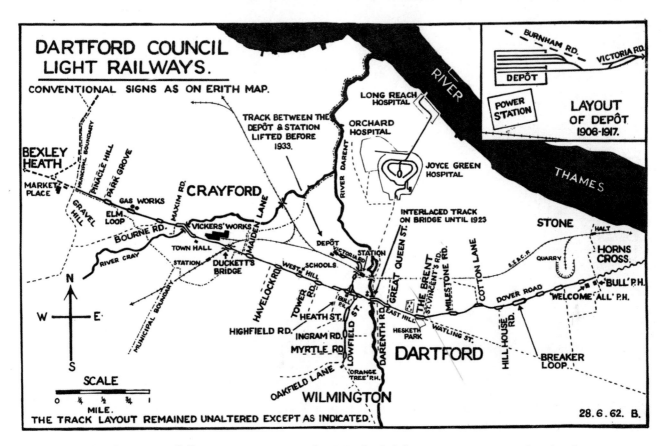

At the turn of the new year 1907 the Woolwich horse trams were beginning to look very much out of place in the modern world. In answer to criticism that the LCC was dragging its feet on electrification, the powers that be cited difficulties in acquiring property for road widening. Further obstacles lay in the way of progress. The reconstruction of the Greenwich to Plumstead line had to be carried out in piecemeal fashion, due to problems of maintaining a service during reconstruction of the permanent way.

Quite simply, new standard gauge tracks had to replace the WSELT narrow gauge ones. On other conversions in the capital it had been possible for horse tramcars to use the new rail infrastructure, as it was prepared for

It is obvious from this picture why several sections of the Woolwich to Abbey Wood route were built with single track. This situation with narrow roads would be sorely tested by an increase in passenger traffic during the First World War. Hold ups to the service could not be tolerated, hence Central Government supplied the finance to replace single with double track at a number of locations. LCC car 178 belongs to class B and has a trolley standard positioned to one side of the top deck. Unusually for this era a motor vehicle has appeared in the shape of a sporting looking run around, registered LD 1709. No doubt the driver is pulling out all the stops to stay ahead of the pursuing tramcar. *Richard Stevenson Collection*

BROADWAY BEXLEYHEATH.

Top deck indicator boxes were fitted from around 1911. The tram route from Bexleyheath to Welling ran along the alignment of the old Roman road, Watling Street. In this view taken some months before the outbreak of the First World War, this was the main highway linking London with the Channel Ports; however, there is still no evidence of any other mechanical transport aside from car 15. *Richard Stevenson Collection*

The notice hanging from the traction bracket arm reads ELECTRIC CARS STOP BY REQUEST. This was all somewhat novel for the people of Belvedere, especially the children, some of whom, ill advisedly, would try to steal a free ride on the fenders of the Erith UDC tramcars. Built new as double track, the route from the town centre to Abbey Wood was engineered in preparation for through running with the LCC, which unfortunately never happened. The exact location of this view is the S bend between Lower Road and Picardy Street. *Richard Stevenson Collection*

1855. BELVEDERE

P.&S. 1331.

Beresford Square, Woolwich would remain the centre of tramway operation for many years. Here at the beginning of the electric era, we observe near the centre of the picture a Bexley car loading for its return journey to Bexleyheath. Meanwhile on the adjacent track an LCC vehicle starts off in the direction of Plumstead and Abbey Wood. Outside the Arsenal main gate a Reckett Smith coal wagon lumbers past. It would be supplying the population with the wherewithal for their winter warmth.

BERESFORD SQUARE, WOOLWICH

On 17th March 1913 eight former horsecars staked another claim to fame. Reconfigured as unpowered trailers, they were sent into operation hitched to standard M class vehicles. Each pair had few problems negotiating the Beresford Square terminal loop, but at the other end by Eltham High Street a neatly choreographed shunting procedure was necessary. Fortunately, there was little other traffic to hinder these manoeuvres. In retrospect this was a bold move by the LCC to increase passenger carrying capacity by the use of coupled units, so popular on the continent of Europe and elsewhere in the world. However, as regards other UK tramway operators the jury was still out as to the effectiveness of trailer cars.

Dartford car 5 awaits departure from Bexleyheath Broadway. Note the splendid condition of the tram, a testament to municipal pride, when vehicles were cleaned daily. When the sun was shining, it was a pleasant experience to enjoy the open air ride from a seat on the upper deck. Note the uniforms of the driver and conductor. The latter sports a leather cash bag and ticket punch. Attached by string to his right lapel is a whistle, which was a legal requirement. Trams were always regarded in law as a form of light railway, hence the conductor's need of a whistle in his role as guard of the vehicle. *Bob Appleton Collection*

We are very fortunate that volunteers and staff of the National Tramway Museum and the LCC Tramways Trust have succeeded in restoring LCC class B car 106 to such a fine state. It is depicted as a member of the fleet serving the Woolwich area. Note the elaborate paint scheme and the lack of external advertising save for a board indicating further tramway connections to North Kent.

M class car 1717 is depicted climbing Well Hall Road, Eltham in the direct of Eltham Common. In a relatively short space of time a country lane has been transformed into a double track tramway with new housing either side of the carriageway. Some of the old field boundary trees, which had probably existed for several hundred years, have been retained. Note the double trolleys on the car, which conformed to the scientific demands of the Astronomer Royal at Greenwich. This section of track was within three miles of the Observatory.

LCC class A car 56 is seen in McLeod Road, Abbey Wood. After the connection was made at Woolwich, larger capacity vehicles could work through from central London. Wartime demands meant the addition of top covered classes A and D to local services. The famous gas lit tram stop sign is partially concealed behind a tree in the centre of the picture. *Richard Stevenson Collection*

This unique, gas lit tram and trolleybus stop once stood on McLeod Road. *Alan Watkins*

109 McLeod Road, Abbey Wood   E.V.B. Series

TRAM TERMINUS ABBEY WOOD

As from New Year's Day 1913 route numbers were allocated to LCC tram services. In the area under review route 42 applied to the line from Woolwich to Abbey Wood; route 44 was displayed on Eltham cars. When the connection was completed to the main system, route 40 was extended to Abbey Wood; route 36 cars reached Woolwich Free Ferry in the evenings; route 38 tramcars terminated at Wickham Lane on Sundays and Saturday afternoons.

The terminus at Abbey Wood was situated adjacent to the county boundary. In fact, the lad to the right of car 1566 is standing in Kent. The vehicle depicted is a member of class E/1, the workhorses of the LCC fleet. The metal EX plate under the canopy edge signifies an extra to the regular service; however, the car is not yet sporting a number stencil in the front upper deck window. A single track connection to Abbey Wood Depot bears to the left behind the tram. *Richard Stevenson Collection*

27

Tram Junction.
Market Place Bexley

Negotiations between Bexley and the LCC caused an alteration to the 38. This change of tack resulted from the latter's desire to conclude through running agreements in the face of increased motor bus competition. As from 11th July 1914, passengers could remain on the LCC car as far as Bexleyheath Broadway. Here on tracks adjacent to the Clock Tower, vehicles from four operators could be seen together. The apple green and cream Erith trams contrasted with shades of maroon on LCC, Bexley and Dartford cars.

British tramway networks in action at Bexleyheath Market Place, as Bexley car 16 shares a track with an Erith double decker. Dartford Council car 12 loads passengers to the right of the clock tower. Again, the complete lack of other motorised traffic is noticeable. *Richard Stevenson Collection*

4 Contrasting Fortunes

Although the London County Council Tramways had been enjoying a period of expansion, other operators in the neighbourhood were experiencing varying fortunes and therefore were obliged to make ends meet as best they could. The principal sufferers in the decade leading up to the First World War were the lines run by Erith Urban District Council. One can only feel a certain amount of sympathy for the elected representatives, who had allocated money and resources to a double track main line from Erith to Abbey Wood, only to be disappointed by the LCC. Vehicles from both councils terminated in sight of one another, but the tracks were not connected. The chance of a potentially lucrative through service went begging.

Erith certainly needed the money. In an effort to cut costs on the Northend route, two single deck, one man operated, demi cars were ordered in 1906. The Erith management may have taken their lead from Gravesend, where two years previously a pair of similar vehicles had entered service on the Dover Road and Windmill Street lines. In the event the Northend branch proved a financial disaster and was shut permanently on 31st August 1910, making it one of the first electric tramway abandonments in London.

The connection to Bexleyheath was also vulnerable, because through running over Bexley metals south of Northumberland Heath had become a sensitive issue. Disagreements over costs incurred by Erith vehicles caused several interruptions to the service. Fortunately, Bexley's attitude to its eastern neighbour was less confrontational and from 27th August 1906 Dartford cars were extended from Gravel Hill to terminate at Bexleyheath Market Place.

The Gravesend management were quick off the mark in instituting economies, when low passenger figures did not justify conventional double deckers on a tram route. The solution appeared to be a single deck demi car, operated by one member of staff. In order to conform with the British left hand rule of the road, the two company employees pictured here are standing next to the front entrance/exit of the vehicle. The trolley rope is tied to the outer casing of the headlamp. Metal plates have been affixed to the top of the fender, in order to deter people hitching an illicit ride on the tramcar.
Bob Appleton Collection

A group waits in the tram shelter for a conveyance to Abbey Wood, whilst car 5 pauses on its journey to Northumberland Heath and the boundary with Bexley tracks. Here outside the Wheatley Arms Hotel was the tramway centre of the town, where the Northend branch joined the main line; a set of points leading to Pier Road was also inserted into the layout, but this line was never completed. *Richard Stevenson Collection*

The outbreak of the First World War on 4th August 1914 had a major impact on all public transport, especially in the Woolwich Area, where thousands were employed in the manufacture of munitions at the Royal Arsenal. Here the tramways came into their own. Temporary 'estates' of wooden huts lined Well Hall Road. Transport to and from these lodgings was supplied by trams and trailers on the Eltham route. Vehicles were packed with men and women engaged on vital war work. Changes in personnel due to male staff joining the armed forces resulted in the employment of women conductors.

All LCC routes passing through Beresford Square experienced an upturn in passenger numbers. The same applied to Bexley cars and to the neighbouring systems at Dartford and Erith. The War Office was particularly keen that workers employed at the various Vickers establishments in Erith, Crayford and Dartford could rely on public transport. There was also pressure on the BET in Gravesend, where the Windmill Street line regained double deckers in preference to demi cars.

Lack of maintenance took its toll on the roadworthiness of the tramcars. Extra vehicles had to be drafted into the area to cope with the upsurge in patronage. Bexley hired cars from the LCC, whilst Erith borrowed two vehicles from Leyton UDC in East London and a further pair of trams from the London United Company. Subsequently, Erith took delivery of an ex Hull bogie car, which arrived by barge from its home town. As a final flourish in an effort to make do and mend, the derelict Northend route was cannibalised for serviceable track components.

Electric trams brought reliable public transport to cities and towns throughout the land. This view represents the heyday of Edwardian suburbia, as car 10 awaits passengers on Bexley Road, Northumberland Heath. Note the sunblinds on the shops, a feature seldom seen in the 21st century. Even though this view dates to over a century ago, the stately Erith double deckers in their attractive apple green livery add an environmentally friendly touch of class to the scene. *Richard Stevenson Collection*

Over in Gravesend the local BET management found conditions difficult. A dearth of spare parts resulted in trams suffering structurally and mechanically. Neglect of bodywork and electrical equipment, plus a number of temporary repairs, gave the fleet a shabby, patched up look and affected the performance of cars especially on hills.

Each system coped with these daily struggles, but worse was to come. The wartime routine in North Kent was rudely interrupted by a disaster in Dartford. In the early hours of Tuesday, 7th August 1917, fire broke out at the depot in Victoria Road and the whole tram fleet went up in smoke. Remarkably the town was without tram services for only twenty-four hours. On Thursday of the same week Bexley vehicles appeared on the streets, working to Wilmington and Horns Cross. Negotiations between the affected parties and officials from the government ensured that workers vital for the war effort could get to their factories by tram.

In order to fill the Dartford void, Bexley took delivery of a further batch of LCC B class tramcars. In the period 1915-1918 a total of 22 of these vehicles joined the fleet. They were allocated the numbers 17-39. Initially acquired on a loan basis, they were later purchased outright. It is fair to say LCC standards of maintenance exceeded those practised by Bexley. Thus the latter gained reliable vehicles, which offered fare paying customers the luxury of a covered top deck.

In Spital Street, Dartford at the junction with Orchard Street the restricted width of the thoroughfare has obliged the council to lay single track. Car 2 makes its way to Bexleyheath past the carriage of one of the wealthier residents of the town. The jumble of architectural styles of the shops and businesses is a joy to behold. This was provincial Britain at the start of the twentieth Century, before the private motor car hijacked town planning. Note the newsagents at the corner of Orchard Street, which supplied local and county newspapers to residents. *Richard Stevenson Collection*

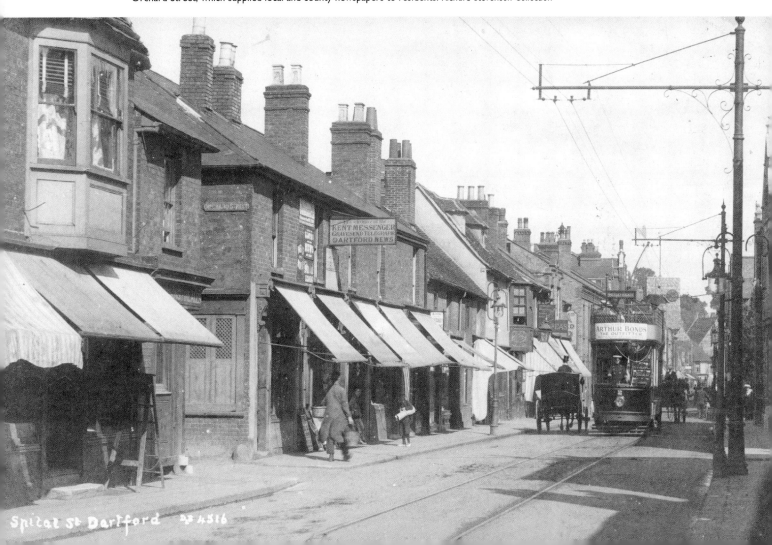

The Bexley Peace Tram is depicted outside the depot. The staff have obviously gone to some trouble the decorate this ex LCC class B car. It is recorded that the vehicle toured the system and was driven by the manager, Mr H.P.Stokes. No doubt he had mixed feelings, because the cessation of hostilities meant the loss to the tramways of the lucrative munitions workers traffic. He was going to face some tough times ahead. *TLRS Archive*

After the Great War ceased in November 1918, those industries connected directly with the manufacture of munitions were run down, thus leading to loss of passenger revenue on the tramways. Indeed, the word 'loss' would figure prominently in subsequent financial accounts of the publicly owned Bexley/Dartford and Erith systems, and the privately run Gravesend & Northfleet. The Company was in greater danger, because the BET was already a stake holder in the North Kent Motor Services, established in 1913. Added to this was the presence of the Maidstone & District Company, whose grip on the area was strengthened in 1920 by the purchase of the North Kent undertaking's motor buses.

In spite of the unsatisfactory state of the Gravesend tramways, the rail bound operation managed to fend off a replacement plan by buses. Internal combustion engine technology had received a boost by developments in military transport during the First World War. It was now perfectly possible for small scale entrepreneurs, many of them ex service men, to band together in order to run a bus route. An obvious target were roads where the trams ran. It was an unfair battle because the mechanised interlopers were not obliged to maintain a fixed infrastructure of rails, roadway and overhead wires.

5 Wretched Little Lines

In a Parliamentary debate on the London Traffic Bill which took place on 24th June 1924, honourable members were discussing 'the power to limit the number of buses plying on certain streets within the City of London and the Metropolitan Police District'.

Members of Parliament were divided between supporters of municipal tramways and those favouring the contemporary 'laissez faire' system of bus routes. John Edmund Mills, Labour MP for Dartford, was acutely aware of shortcomings in public transport and their effect on his constituents. Mr Mills was an engineer employed at the Royal Arsenal and a former member of Woolwich Borough Council. He was especially critical of the LCC attitude to Erith:

Mr Mills....It is merely that if you look at the Manchester Corporation tramway service, operating in very narrow streets with a success which is remarkable, it is due to the fact that they have not had to end their termini at bottle necks and are given the opportunity of circular roads, which are denied to us. Take my own Division. We have the County Council tramway cars ending at Abbey Wood. The Erith Council Tramways begin there, and their vehicles go round to Bexley Heath Broadway....There they end, and the Erith Council admittedly bears a loss on its rates and will not give up its power of owning these trams. From there they run back in a circle and complete the circle through Erith and Bexley Heath back to Abbey Wood - two separate urban authorities running two wretched little lines of tramways, both bearing a loss on the rates, and all due to limited powers which have been conferred on the County Council.

A schoolboy peers out from the top deck, as the motorman slows Bexley car 24 with the hand brake. This tramcar was acquired second hand from the LCC and is photographed en route for Horns Cross. This is a classic view of the tramway era in North Kent. Note the local advertising for the films at the Palace Cinema, Bexleyheath. Also on view on the bulkhead of the lower saloon is the MSC plate number 2131.

In spite of the travails of the neighbouring local authorities, the London County Council continued with an expansionist policy in the post war years. Here at the corner of High Street, Plumstead and Griffin Road, trams on routes 40 and 38 pass. E/1 class car 1480 heads for Victoria Embankment in the heart of the capital. In the spring of 1928 the single through fare for a journey of 76 minutes on routes 36/38 was 5d and the return was a bargain 8d. *Richard Stevenson Collection*

The BET owned Gravesend company sought to enhance revenues by hiring out advertising spaces on their tramcars. Some of this work was skilfully crafted manually by sign writers; metal enamelled plates on the top deck decency boards were provided by commercial enterprises wanting to promote their wares. We observe the silver wheel and magnet device of the British Electric Traction Company at the centre of the waist panel. Other features of note are the reversed stairs and the detail of the Brill 21E truck, as used throughout the tramway world. *Bob Appleton Collection*

It will come as no surprise to the reader that the municipal lines run by Bexley and Erith continued to record poor financial results. Operations had to be subsidised by ratepayers, until, theoretically, economies could be made. Little or no provision had been made for fleet renewals. In reality this was hardly an effective approach; however, the 'make do and mend' strategy, already in operation since before the First World War, reached new heights of ingenuity. Both undertakings would eventually survive incorporation into the LPTB in the summer of 1933. However, that is to get ahead of our story.

The working arrangement between Bexley Council Tramways and Dartford Light Railways was formalised by an accord, which was to take effect from 1st April 1921. A joint committee was formed; Balfour, Beatty & Co relinquished their interest in the Dartford network. Following this agreement, there was a short term uplift in the tramways' fortunes. It was always maintained that the section between Bexleyheath and Woolwich was profitable. Unfortunately, the same could not be said for the rest of the system. One can only speculate on the positive financial benefits, if the connection from Horns Cross to Swanscombe had been built. As it was, competing buses filled the gap, thus robbing the trams of passengers.

In July 1924 Erith approached the LCC with a request for what would now be called a 'rescue package' to save the town's tramways. Three years previously the London County Council had taken over the Leyton network, much to the relief of the local authority in East London. Whether it was a case of 'once bitten, twice shy' for the policy makers in County Hall, we cannot be certain, but the outcome for Erith was disappointment. Even though the Ministry of Transport had expressed hopes of a regeneration of the North West Kent tramways, there were no government funds available. The LCC demurred and nothing came of the proposal. The trams were living on borrowed time. The Ministry of Transport official statistics recorded tramcars owned at 31st December 1928 and financial information at the end of the fiscal year 1928/29:

London County Council Tramways
Total Income £4,315,214
Total Working Expenses £3,615,419
Mileage of Lines. Total Route Length 166.28
Total Number of Cars in Stock 1,817
Passengers Carried 713,035,141
Traffic Income per Car Mile 14.62d
Working Expenditure per Car Mile 12.38d

Bexley Tramways & Dartford Light Railways Joint Committee
Total Income £55,872
Total Working Expenses £45,332
Mileage of Lines. Total Route Length 10.29
Total Number of Cars in Stock 33
Passengers Carried 8,053,795
Traffic Income per Car Mile 18.22d
Working Expenditure per Car Mile 15.01d

Erith Urban District Council
Total Income £24,397
Total Working Expenses £26,048
Mileage of Lines. Total Route Length 5.42
Total Number of Cars in Stock 19
Passengers Carried 5,371,644
Traffic Income per Car Mile 15.27d
Working Expenditure per Car Mile 18.45d

Gravesend and Northfleet
Total Income £21,297
Total Working Expenses £18,398
Mileage of Lines. Total Route Length 6.47
Total Number of Cars in Stock 18
Passengers Carried 4,304,231
Traffic Income per Car Mile 10.62d
Working Expenditure per Car Mile 9.32d

Erith entered the second hand market in order to bolster the rolling stock. This was a classic strategy of make do and mend, for the council had precious little funds to invest in its tramway system. Acquired from Hull Corporation, car 19 was nicknamed 'the tank' by the crews. This substantial looking vehicle served its purpose, but could be temperamental on the less than perfect Erith track. Other drawbacks included the fact that it was heavy on current and was banned from working to Bexleyheath.

The first casualty of the 1920s was Gravesend. In spite of valiant efforts to maintain a transport system that was showing its age, at the end of 1928 the BET indicated it was about to transfer ownership of the tramways to the Maidstone & District Motor Services Ltd. The abandonment of the local trams was perceived as part of the natural order of things. The last cars ran on 28th February 1929. A bargain sale of tram bodies then followed. Covered top vehicles could be purchased at £10 each; a fiver sufficed for the open toppers. Trucks and electrical equipment were scrapped. Folk with enough cash and garden space could now store their spades, forks and flower pots in one of the best products Brush of Loughborough could supply in the first decade of the century. *O Tempora, O Mores!*

Thus, Gravesend had the dubious honour of being the first electric tramway in the Greater London area to start an abolitionist movement, which would end on 5th July 1952. In the nation as a whole the years following the Wall Street Crash of autumn 1929 were known as the Great Depression. This expression could equally be applied to the mood of tram enthusiasts in London and elsewhere. The writing was on the wall, when the findings of the Royal Commission on Transport were published in 1931. It was recommended that no more tramways should be built and those remaining should be replaced by other forms of transport.

August Bank Holiday traditionally fell on the first Monday of the month. Although tram crews were obliged to maintain the service, most of the rest of the working population took the chance to enjoy some leisure time. This evocative scene taken around 1930 features car 28 as it clatters over the triangular junction in the centre of Dartford. Two gents in flat caps are clutching bags of chips, while on the opposite side of the road the Bull Hotel offers a more expensive choice of luncheons and teas. *H.Wightman/A.J.Watkins*

The end of the line at Horns Cross, the most easterly point of the London tramway network, has been reached by Bexley car 30. The former Gravesend tramways were only a mile or so further on. Woolwich was just over an hour and a quarter away, although it is unlikely anyone but a hardened tram enthusiast would have made the complete journey. This being a very rural location, illumination at night for conductors putting the trolley on the wire was supplied by a bank of three light bulbs suspended above the overhead. Today this former tram terminus lies outside the M25 London Orbital Motorway.

The only operator to counter this trend was the LCC. Even members of the Royal Commission acknowledged the tramcar's ability to shift large crowds in cities, where an intensive service could be offered. The two Metropolitan Boroughs of Woolwich and Lewisham were still very pro tram. In this spirit of cooperation the County Council planned new housing estates with tramway connections to the centre of London.

Before this could be achieved, some loose ends were tidied up. On 22nd March 1921 a connection on the overhead wire system was opened between Lee Green and the former Eltham terminus outside St.John's Church. Locals could now avail themselves of service 46 from Beresford Square to Southwark Bridge. The number 44 was retained for short workings from Woolwich to Eltham Church. This was a natural traffic route with heavy passenger loadings.

At the behest of Woolwich Borough Council further expansion plans were being considered. Former farm land to the south of the borough was marked out for local authority housing. A tramway to serve the influx of new residents was projected from Grove Park to a junction with existing tracks at the Yorkshire Grey, Eltham Green. A further section was planned to bypass Eltham town centre. It would include a connection to routes 44 and 46 at Well Hall roundabout. Westhorne Avenue was constructed with a tramway, which opened in its entirety on 30th June 1932. Route 72 was diverted to run from Victoria Embankment, Savoy Street to Beresford Square. Sadly, this new section of street track was the last throw of the dice for the LCC, before the arrival of the LPTB in July 1933.

6 Memories of a Tram Driver

In the early 1970s, your author met George Tapp, a retired, former Erith tram driver. Motorman Tapp was happy to give several interviews about aspects of his working life:

I worked as a tram driver for the Erith tramways. It was a steady job. I was lucky to have it during the years of the Depression in the late 1920s and early 1930s. The effects of unemployment were far worse in other parts of the country away from the London area. So, although there was real poverty among working people, we got by because there was always some work to be had, even if it meant travelling from your home. The workmen's fares on the trams were a godsend and I know from my own family that, when the munitions factories laid off people after the First World War, the men at least found jobs in Woolwich or in the building trade, when they were putting up new housing estates in the Eltham and Sidcup areas.

Having said all that, the workforce that kept the trams running in Erith was the salt of the earth. We didn't get much money as regards wages. They were lower than the amount LCC drivers and conductors received. In fact I later found out we were bottom of the pay scales for tramway workers in the metropolitan region. In spite of this, the morale among my workmates was good. Basically, we knew our employer was the local authority with little spare cash, not some private company out for profit. If they had been a private company they would have closed down the tramways years before, because quite frankly the finances of Erith UDC Tramways were lousy!

This was one of the pictures to which George Tapp is referring. What a wonderful array of local bigwigs in all their Edwardian finery! This social gathering heralds the start of a municipal enterprise, which the council hoped would prove lucrative. Sadly, reality soon set in; by the time this image was on the depot wall in the late 1920s, irreverent members of staff had christened it the 'Toffs & Burlington Bertie' photo. I'll leave the reader to decide who most qualifies for the latter role. *Richard Stevenson Collection*

You could say, we supplied public transport on a shoe string. The philosophy was very much 'make do and mend' and this attitude meant that everyone from mechanics, fitters, conductors and drivers to overhead line crews and clerical people shared skills. By that I mean, if something went wrong and the service was interrupted there was no rigid division of 'who does what', we all mucked in together to get the trams running again. Passengers appreciated us and when the power failed or there was a derailment, very few people moaned or complained to the management. After all, the local ratepayers actually owned the tramway, even if it had definitely seen better days.

You've seen pictures of the system when it opened in August 1905 with everyone looking smart and all the bigwigs from the council decked out in their finery. In those days the cars were painted a light shade of apple green with primrose round the windows and rocker panels. They must have looked very smart.

What a contrast to the trams I drove. They'd all been repainted a dark brown colour. I do remember someone found some tins of the original green lurking somewhere in a corner of the depot. I think they were concealed under a tarpaulin. By that time, it must have been around Christmas 1930, I was union rep at the depot. Several of us came up with the idea of repainting one of the cars in 1905 condition. The intention was to parade it around the streets at a suitable civic festival or charity fund raising event. It never got done, but the paint was still there, when the Board (London Passenger Transport Board) took over in 1933. Of course, the new regime had no intention of using anything but red!

My work day started at the depot in Walnut Tree Road. As a driver you had to check everything was in working order on the tram. If one of the fitters had done some maintenance on your car, he either put a note on the controller or spoke to you before his shift knocked off. My main concern was always that the brakes were working and after that, before I left the depot, I used to cross my fingers that I wouldn't have any electrical problems or a derailment on the road.

Speeds were low. Catching an Erith tram was faster than walking, though not by much! The track was bad in some places, but the four wheelers, the single truck trams, usually coped quite well. If any problems did arise, you could bet your bottom dollar it was one of the eight wheel, bogie cars that was playing up. I think we had six of those in the fleet. One from Hull and the others ex LUT open top vehicles from West London. Several times when driving them, I came off the rails in West Street by the level crossings. Luckily with help of some passengers and some nifty manoeuvres from yours truly, coaxing the car gently back on the track, we were able to get to Abbey Wood and deliver people to their work on time.

Talking of speed reminds me of a funny incident. There were time clocks at various places. The one at Abbey Wood used to record arrivals and departures on a printed roll of paper. Tram crews had a key, although the conductor usually operated the thing. These paper rolls were then examined by the clerical staff back at HQ. From time to time they were displayed with the name of the driver on each roll. Occasionally, when time keeping wasn't

Erith did find the cash to rebuild the stairs and front canopies of all four former London United trams acquired second hand from West London. Seating 74, they were good crowd shifters, but lacking top covers they gave a grim ride in inclement weather. Their usefulness was also restricted by a regular tendency to derail at the level crossings in West Street. Consequently, motormen kept the speed down and these vehicles got a reputation as 'crawlers'.

what it should have been, the management got the notion they would try to shame the slow coaches among us. This sounded a bit like victimisation to me and as union rep I wasn't having any of it. However humour took the sting out of the situation. We had one particularly slow driver. I suppose you could say he was over cautious. Someone had crossed out his name on the roll and put in big letters MALCOLM CAMPBELL on it. He was the one who held several land speed records in the 1920s and 1930s. We all had a good laugh then.

Back on the run to Abbey Wood, the other thing you had to watch out for was vehicles running away down the hill from Upper Belvedere at the S bend leading to Belvedere Station. Several of my mates had near misses. Once a steam wagon got out of control, careered across the tram tracks, then headed along Station Road and wrecked the gates at the level crossing. No doubt the Southern Railway had something to say about that! We probably benefited, because with the train service out of action, we'd have picked up more passengers from Erith town centre to Abbey Wood.

I also drove on the line to Bexleyheath Broadway or the Market Place or the Clock Tower, as it was known. It was single track and loops all the way. At Northumberland Heath our tracks ended and the Bexley metals began. They were almost in the same boat as we were regarding finances and the track was equally poor on their territory as it was on ours. Still, in the summer it was a nice leisurely ride with fields and bits of open countryside, before the houses were built. Near Courtleet Bottom there was a line of bushes and trees. Several times on the return trip to Erith my conductor 'rang off' the car and darted into the foliage to relieve himself! You have to remember in those days crew facilities and comforts were minimal and meal breaks were taken on the hoof, as it were. All that changed, of course, with the arrival of London Transport and better conditions for staff.

Every summer at the end of July we had Bexley Gala Day at Danson Park. We then would take our trams through to the park. Just past the Clock Tower there was a connecting line to the main Bexley tracks. The points and the point blades were out of alignment and bent at an angle. You had to creep across them, hoping that you made it without coming off. Once clear of them it was a straight run to Crook Log. Because of the single track and loops layout, you had to shuttle backwards and forwards to let service cars past.

Obviously we chatted to our Bexley colleagues. I knew many of them due to my work with the union. I must say they were a conservative bunch, with a big and little C. Normally you didn't talk politics or religion much, except in the company of like minded folk. But we used to tease the Bexley crews by pointing out the motto on the Erith coat of arms, which read 'Labour Overcomes All Things'. And, thinking about it now, I suppose Erith Council Tramways was the nearest public transport in London came to a socialist cooperative. Unity was certainly strength in those days.

As already related, much of the local trackwork had seen better days. Rail joints were split, granite setts had sunk in the roadway and tramcars ran on their flanges at locations, where the permanent way had drifted out of gauge. Here at Bexleyheath Broadway it took some skill to negotiate the misaligned connecting track with the main line. No wonder LPTB engineers were alarmed at the state of the tramlines on their first visits in early 1933. *H. Wightman/A.J. Watkins*

In the early 1930s it was obvious the writing was on the wall as far as the local tramways were concerned. Rumours started to circulate that the council were going to cut their losses and throw us all out of a job. As union rep I was worried and I arranged to meet other union people from Bexley, the LCC and across London, as well as the bus people, who incidentally were better paid than tram crews.

Eventually, it became clear a grand scheme was being concocted in Parliament, and, as you know, the LPTB took over in July 1933. Even then the rumours kept coming. There were real fears we were going to be shut down and the routes given over to the green country bus department. Nobody mentioned trolleybuses at first, but they later came into the discussion, after news reached us of the success of the London United conversions in West London.

Before that, if I remember right, a couple of my mates got hold of an old military motorcycle and sidecar to go off and visit trolleybus installations. They must have been good mechanics, because the bike was held together with bits of wire! However, they did manage to get to Hastings, Southend and Maidstone in one piece. They talked to the crews and sampled the new vehicles for themselves. When we chatted about it afterwards, it appeared trolleybuses were being used successfully to replace tramcars. Which was hardly surprising if you compared an old open top tram with the latest all enclosed trolleybus.

So we were very relieved when we found out that the Board were going to put trolleybuses on our local routes. We'd heard horror stories of people

At Bexleyheath Broadway George Tapp takes a rest break before the return to Abbey Wood. He now works for a large, powerful organisation and has relatively secure employment with the LPTB, even though his new bosses lack the 'matey' atmosphere of the old Erith UDC Tramways.

losing their jobs when M&D (Maidstone & District Motor Services) buses took over from the trams in Gravesend. I was determined not to let anything like that happen to us after July 1933, when the Board took over.

To say things were hectic in the first few months of control from 55 Broadway, SW1 (HQ of the LPTB) is rather an understatement. At the end of June 1933, I'd organised a farewell bash for all of my Erith colleagues. Then we all crossed our fingers hoping our new employers were going to treat us properly. We need not have worried. We got a pay rise and staff conditions improved under the new regime. They also brought in new trams. As you know, they were four wheelers of the M class from ex LCC stock. I forget all their numbers now, but they pretty soon replaced most of the old Bexley and Erith fleets.

I did feel rather sad to see them being towed or driven away. Just so much scrap metal, but nothing lasts for ever. What was good, was the fact crews benefited from getting rid of the open toppers. In Winter when the wind and rain swept in from the Thames, it was miserable. Sometimes when we came up the slope to the railway bridge in Lower Road, you could feel the full force of the icy weather, as it hit the tram. No windscreens in those days, of course. You needed a thick coat and gloves to stay warm, as well as goggles to keep the sleet out of your eyes!

Erith Depot was closed in 1934 and the trams were shifted to Abbey Wood Depot. The Board had put in a single track connection on Knee Hill, so that we could get cars in and out on to route 98, as it became. To begin with, there was a sort of 'them and us' atmosphere at Abbey Wood. The old LCC crews definitely thought we were a bunch of interlopers, as it were. They weren't too complimentary about our trams. But things settled down later. Still, I did have to put up with the Abbey Wood lot, until we got trolleybuses and our new depot at the back end of 1935.

One of the things that did change with the Board was that I got the chance to drive on route 96 from Woolwich to Dartford. I drove not only the main road, but a few weeks before it closed, I took an M class car down the Wilmington branch. The track there was really ropey, I can tell you. It was a proper 'wing and prayer' job. No wonder the Board closed it.

People have written that we could only run the M class at half power. Not strictly true, because, where the track was in better condition and there were fewer people wanting to get on or off, and no inspectors about, you could get up some speed. When you were used to driving an older type of car, the ride on an M was a bit different. They were solidly constructed, but the whole bodywork seemed to move together in several directions, backwards, forwards and sideways! I can only describe the motion as 'bouncing'. Of course, this wasn't so bad for the passengers, because they had upholstered seats to sit on, not like the hard wooden benches we had at Erith.

In my job as union rep I did get to meet Thomas (T.E.Thomas, LPTB General Manager Trams & Trolleybuses). It was as much as he could do to listen to me, as I told him of the concerns of my members. He was pretty rude about the state of our local tramways. He criticised the track and said that the overhead was 'like washing line'. I didn't take to him at all and the feeling was mutual. It was like being patronised by a boss, who had little idea what his workers did. But to be fair to the bloke, he did confirm that we would keep our jobs, when the trolleybuses came in. He did tell me the trolleybuses we were getting would be similar to those already operating with the London United in West London.

Thomas was true to his word. In the summer of 1935 the overhead wire crews arrived. They started at Abbey Wood and worked their way round. They installed new traction standards along the route. Just about all the old Erith poles had almost rusted away by then. As the trolleybus overhead went up, we were meant to use one wire of it. I believe the original intention was not to erect any extra tram overhead, but at a number of places, Crook Log is one I recall, there was temporary wiring we tram drivers could use.

The new LPTB trolleybus depot was constructed as a stylish 1930s building on what was once a potato field at the boundary of Crayford UDC. This was George's home for the rest of his working life with London Transport. It is depicted here a couple of months after trolleybuses supplanted trams in the area. Contractors are still engaged on putting the finishing touches to the structure. *London Transport Museum U19647/Mick Webber Collection*

After the builders got going on the new trolleybus depot, we had a spell of around three months to get familiar with the set up. When the wires were being finished, each driver had a week's training around the depot and eventually out on the road. I took the first trolleybus from Bexleyheath to Abbey Wood and back. On the stretch from Abbey Wood to Woolwich Ferry, there was originally no third wire in McLeod Road to pass trams. There was a very tight turning circle at Abbey Wood. On the trolleybuses the steering lock was good when new, but it got stiff after visiting Charlton Works.

That turning circle on Knee Hill, Abbey Wood was a sort of showpiece for the management. The Board brought parties of transport people, including foreigners, to see it. We heard a rumour that a party from Moscow had

inspected it. It seems Uncle Joe (Stalin) had trolleybus plans for the Soviet Union. Thomas made it quite clear to me, when we met, that the Board was 'a business, not a workers' cooperative like in Russia!' I wonder if the bigwigs at the LPTB said that to the Soviets, when they were showing them round?

Of course, we shed a few tears when the trams finished, but to be honest, passengers loved the new trolleybuses and, as a driver, I had a nice comfortable cab rather than an open platform exposed to all weathers. And I got to sit down at work! We didn't have to put up with single track and loops, which slowed down the tram service; it was a lot safer on Bexley Road, Erith, where they had widened the road, but left the track on the right hand side. As motor traffic increased, there were some nasty near misses on that section with trams going against the flow.

As you know, the section from Dartford centre to Horns Cross was abandoned and the country bus people ran the replacement service. In the war there was a rumour the Board were going to extend the trolleybuses in that direction, but nothing came of it.

There are two things which stand out in those early years of the trolleybuses. We had a rather eccentric driver also called George, but I forget his last name. He was the one who dumped his bus in a front garden on Wickham Lane. I've got a feeling it was in December 1936. My second memory of this time was driving the first seventy seater. Leyland Motors had sent an official photographer and they gave me a copy of the photo. We needed those bigger vehicles, because of the increase in passengers on both the 'sixes' and the 'eights' (routes 696 & 698).

I know we had better conditions of employment and fringe benefits with the Board. Bexleyheath Trolleybus Depot was a clean, modern place with up to date facilities for crews and vehicles. It was quite a contrast with both Erith and Bexley tram depots. We certainly got the best deal there. But, what the Board lacked was a family atmosphere. The human element was not the same as it was in Erith....

Parked opposite West Hill Schools, Dartford, George Tapp awaits further instructions. He was honoured to be the first driver chosen to take the new seventy seater Leyland, class D1 384, for a spin out along route 696. These vehicles offered great seating capacity to cope with the influx of new passengers. The small poster extolling the virtues of the Green Line, reminds us that Dartford was very much country bus territory. *BCVM 26.6.36/Mick Webber Collection*

7 The LPTB and Trolleybus...

The state of the local roads had been discussed in high places. Mr Mills, MP for Dartford, aired the matter in the House of Commons in a debate on 19th November 1930:

Mr Mills asked the Minister of Transport if he is aware of the dangerous state of the main road from Woolwich to Bexley, known as Wickham Hill, which is still without a footpath on its most dangerous bend, and if, in view of recurring damage to tramcars and other vehicles, he will order a local inquiry?

The Minister, Herbert Morrison MP, did not think an inquiry was necessary, but promised to bring the situation to the attention of the local authority.

Out on the road south of Northumberland Heath, Bexley car 11 has been drafted in as a works car for the permanent way department. It is towing the Bexley flat truck, a four wheel platform pressed into service to carry some of the workers' tools needed to repair the worn rails and associated paving. There is no sign here of any mechanical aids. The road squad had to put up with picks, shovels and wheelbarrows. Note the rural aspect before the 1930s suburban housing boom.

36/38 Abbey Wood - New Cross - Embankment
          via Woolwich, Charlton, Greenwich, New Cross,
          Old Kent Road, Bricklayers Arms, Elephant,
          Blackfriars Bridge (36) or Westminster Bridge (38)

          Service Interval. 2-4 mins. Journey Time 70 mins.
          Through Fare 5d.

40 Abbey Wood - New Cross - Embankment
          via Woolwich, Charlton, Greenwich, New Cross, Peckham, Camberwell,
          Kennington, Kennington Road, Westminster Bridge, Embankment.

          Service Interval. 4-10 mins. Journey Time 75 mins.
          Through Fare 5d.

44 Woolwich - Shooters Hill - Eltham
          Service Interval. Weekdays Only 8-10 mins.
          Journey Time 18 mins. Through Fare 3d.

46 Woolwich (Beresford Square) - Southwark
          via Shooters Hill, Well Hall Road, Eltham High Street,
          Lee Green, Lewisham, New Cross, Old Kent Road,
          Bricklayers Arms, Great Dover Street, Southwark Bridge.

          Service Interval 4-10 mins. Journey Time 64 mins.
          Through Fare 5d.

72 Woolwich - New Cross - Embankment
          via Shooters Hill, Westhorne Avenue, Lee,
          Lewisham, New Cross, Peckham, Camberwell,
          Kennington, Westminster Bridge.

          Service Interval 8-10 mins. Journey Time 70 mins.
          Through Fare 5d.

96 Woolwich - Dartford - Horns Cross
          via Plumstead, Wickham Lane, Welling, Bexleyheath,
          Dover Road, Crayford.

          Service Interval. Woolwich - Dartford (St.Vincents Road)
          6-12 mins. Dartford - Horns Cross 10-24 mins.
          Journey Time 76 mins. Through Fare 8d.

98 Abbey Wood - Bexleyheath
          via Abbey Road, Belvedere, Erith, Pier Road,
          Northumberland Heath, Bexley Road.

          Through Fare 4d. Service Interval 6-10 mins.
          Journey Time 34 mins.

In practice there were numerous short workings on tram services and this aspect of the timetable would continue with the replacing trolleybuses.

The London Passenger Transport Act of 31st July 1934 contained 120 paragraphs with many clauses. Amongst other things it paved the way for the trolleybus conversion of the erstwhile Erith, Bexley and Dartford tram systems. In paragraph 55(e) the Board sought powers to erect 'a tramcar and trolley vehicle depot in the urban district of Crayford'.

This was a logical step, because both the Erith and Bexleyheath tram depots were deemed unsuitable for reconstruction. The future trolleybus depot would later take shape in the spring of 1935 on the east side of Erith Road, Bexleyheath, just a few yards within the boundary of Crayford Urban District Council. In spite of the official wording of the Act, no tram rails were ever laid in the new structure. There was a rumour among staff that two temporary sidings were originally envisaged. In the event such a provision was not necessary and agreement was reached with Bexley Council over the continued use of their former tram sheds, before UDC dust carts took possession of the building!

Evidence of the newer form of electric traction became apparent from the summer of 1935, when overhead wire crews descended on the area. In fact, because of the decayed state of traction standards and associated wiring, there was a clean sweep of all the electrical infrastructure needed for the conversion. During the transition period, trams used one wire of the trolleybus overhead; however, some temporary wiring was necessary along Bexley Road, Erith, Crook Log and Parkview Road, Welling.

After training personnel to operate the tram replacement vehicles, the great day dawned on Sunday 10th November 1935, when trolleybuses on route 698 took up service from Bexleyheath to Woolwich via Erith and Abbey Wood. This was followed two weeks later by the introduction on 24th November of route 696 from Woolwich to Dartford via Welling, Bexleyheath and Crayford. On the section between Abbey Wood and Woolwich tramcars and trolleybuses worked over the same roads. LPTB observers had been conducting passenger surveys on trams travelling eastwards from Dartford. The evidence indicated that it would be uneconomic to extend trolleybuses to Horns Cross; therefore, country bus route 480 supplied replacement vehicles.

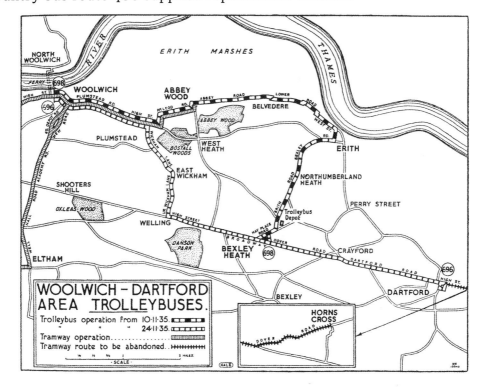

55

With the indicator blind already changed for the return trip, class D1 384 (CUL 384) is depicted on its inaugural run to Woolwich, as it traverses Beresford Square in June 1936. The main gate of the Royal Arsenal dominates the scene. Trams will continue to serve this location until July 1952 and trolleybuses until March 1959. *BCVM/Mick Webber Collection*

57

In the centre of Woolwich there had been some debate concerning the location of a suitable turning circle for the trolleybuses. Beresford Square and the adjacent streets, where trams conformed to a one way system, were considered for the terminus of routes 696 and 698. The proposal failed, because it was felt the already intensive tram service on routes 44, 46 and 72 would cause delays for the trolleybuses. In the end, a rather cramped arrangement at the top of Market Hill, a few yards distant from the Free Ferry Approach, had to suffice. A fleet of 38 vehicles were rostered from Bexleyheath Depot. Each class B2 trolleybus seated 32 in the upper saloon and 28 in the lower.

As well as introducing more trolleybuses, the LPTB was now responsible for a large operating area, which included Gravesend within its boundaries. There were, of course, no trams to be taken into ownership. Their memory lived on at the former depot buildings on Dover Road, which were acquired by the Board. This site had space for fifty-seven buses in total, with covered accommodation for twenty-seven vehicles. On 7th July 1937 it was replaced by the new Northfleet Garage.

Although the intention to replace all London's tramways became official policy, it was imperative to keep the rail bound network in good order pending the introduction of the trackless form of electric traction. Logically, access to the Central Repair Works at Charlton needed to be maintained, until the conclusion of the conversion programme. It was estimated this process would be complete by circa 1942.

On 25th March 1934 car 1103 derailed and overturned in Eltham. Instead of writing off the wreck, Charlton Works installed a new domed roof, driver's vestibules and modernised seating. In the next few months the staff at Charlton were engaged in similar tasks as part of the reconstruction

The Woolwich trolleybus terminus was situated on Market Hill within walking distance of the Free Ferry approach road. Note the new passenger shelter, cantilevered to cope with the slope of the pavement. Class B2 113 (CGF 113) turns the heads of the onlookers; it is in sparkling condition, complete with silver painted roof. *London Transport Museum*

Trolleybuses always appeared somewhat ungainly, when reversing with the trolley poles in the 'wrong' direction. Here at Princes Road, Crayford, the driver of class H1 786B (ELB 786) watches the speed as he endeavours not to dewire his vehicle. This was originally a battery reversal point, but was wired up during the war. It catered for nearby factory workers. This vehicle will work as a 698 to Erith. *Alan Cross*

programme for tramcars. A number of these rehabilitated or 'rehab' vehicles appeared in the Woolwich area. It is fair to say they were seen as a short term stop gap, until trolleybuses could take over across the metropolitan area.

Suburban housebuilding in the 1930s in Barnehurst, Welling, Bexleyheath, Crayford and Dartford ensured more passengers for the already popular trolleybus services. Retail establishments received a boost by new customers being brought to the front door. The situation demanded larger vehicles with greater seating capacity to cope with the crowds. From the spring of 1936 a number of D2 class trolleybuses were drafted in to assist.

Increased motor traffic at the junction of Eltham Road, Westhorne Avenue and Eltham Hill obliged the authorities to install a gyratory system, which was operational from 25th August 1935. Trams conformed to the flow, thus necessitating new automatic points, which in theory at least would save crews alighting from their trams in order to employ a point iron. In practice just over twice as many trams ran on services 44EX and 46 than went via Westhorne Avenue on route 72, therefore it often fell to motormen on the latter route to check the right of way before proceeding.

In tram days fluctuations in traffic levels had resulted in a number of short workings, whereby journeys were curtailed to ensure a more intensive service on certain sections of the route. Whereas a tramcar, being double ended, could reverse easily, a suitable turning circle had to be erected for trolleybuses. In the case of Springfield Road, Welling a backstreet loop, opened on 6th February 1938, provided a much needed reversal point. This was not the end of the process, because in the same year 'battery turns' at Griffin Road, Plumstead and at Princes Road, Crayford were approved by the Ministry of Transport. Initially these locations were not wired up; each trolleybus had to reverse employing battery power.

Another turning circle had been provided at Walnut Tree Road, Erith. This facility was used by vehicles on route 694, introduced on Sunday 16th May 1937, which operated on Sunday and Bank Holiday afternoons and evenings. It linked Erith with Woolwich via Bexleyheath and Welling.

Winter Timetable 1937-38

36/38 Abbey Wood - Victoria Embankment

> Single 5d. Return 8d. Time 73 mins.
> Service 2-4 mins.

40 Woolwich (Beresford Square) - Victoria Embankment

> (Savoy Street) - Extended to Wickham Lane Weekday Peak Hours.
> Single 5d. Return 8d. Time 60 mins.
> Service 4-10 mins.

44 Woolwich (Beresford Square) – Eltham. Weekdays Only.

> Single 3d. Return 5d. Time 18 mins.
> Service 8-10 mins.

46 Woolwich (Beresford Square) - City (Southwark)

> Single 5d. Return 8d. Time 64 mins.
> Service 4-10 mins.

72 Woolwich (Beresford Square) - Victoria Embankment (Savoy Street)

> Single 5d. Return 8d. Time 70 mins.
> Service 8-10 mins.

696 Woolwich (Free Ferry) - Dartford (Market Street)

> Single 8d. Return 1/-. Time 45 mins.
> Service 4-8 mins.

Additional Service 694 on Sunday Afternoons and Evenings Between Woolwich and Erith Via Welling and Bexleyheath.

698 Woolwich (Free Ferry) – Bexleyheath

> Single 7d. Return 11d. Time 43 mins.
> Service 6-10 mins.

In the summer of 1937 there was considerable agitation among some residents of Eltham in response to LPTB plans for trolleybus wiring in several side streets. Householders in Sherard Road and Lassa Road were distinctly unimpressed by the idea of their suburban idyll being spoiled by 'festoons of overhead wires'. The fact that the Board were allegedly pushing schemes through 'willy-nilly' left a bad taste in the mouths of locals. The imposition of Bexleyheath trolleybus depot on 'a quiet neighbourhood' was cited as evidence of the Board's dictatorial approach. In Eltham there was actually quite a pro-tram feeling and this may account for some of the hostility.

The year 1938 saw the second penetration of the trolleybus within the Metropolitan Borough of Woolwich. On Sunday, 6th February vehicles on route 669 reached the north bank of the Thames adjacent to the Free Ferry terminal. There had never been a tramway at this location; the arrival of electric traction at North Woolwich represented the longest LPTB trolleybus extension over previous tramless roads. Trolleybuses ceased here on 3rd February 1960.

Certainly, no lingering doubt remained about the future. The fate of the South London network had been sealed; however, a spanner was thrown in the works from an source outside the control of 55 Broadway - the Third Reich. After war was declared on 3rd September 1939, other more pressing transport priorities emerged. In June 1940 the trolleybus conversion programme was halted in its tracks in East London. The system south of the Thames including trams on routes 36, 38, 40, 44, 46 and 72 was granted a reprieve.

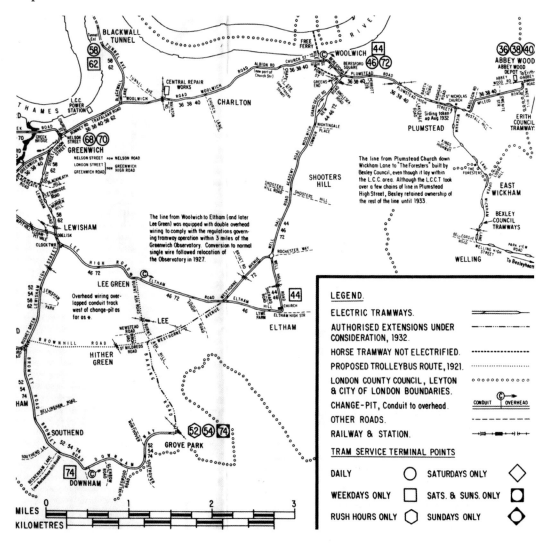

8 Under Fire

The Second World War had a lasting impact on the civilian population of South East London and North West Kent. Enemy air raids from the autumn of 1940 caused significant casualties and damage to property. On 9th September an unexploded bomb (UXB) at Well Hall Roundabout interrupted services 44, 46 and 72 for three days. Unfortunately, on 12th of the month Plumstead sub station was also hit. This affected all local trams and trolleybuses and something approximating normal service could not be restored until twelve days later.

The area was again targeted on 15th September, when high explosive bombs damaged tracks on Well Hall Road, Eltham Common. An emergency bus service from Woolwich to Eltham was necessary, although buses had to make diversions along side streets. On 18th of the same month Woolwich Road was impassable for trams coming from Greenwich. Two days later blast damage brought down overhead wires at Well Hall Roundabout. They had been repaired from the incident earlier in the month.

'Keep Calm & Carry On' is the spirit evoked by this view of bomb damage at Abbey Wood Depot. Since this was after the Luftwaffe raiders had departed, one wonders what possible role the member of the LPTB home guard, complete with rifle and tin hat, had to perform. Maybe he represents defiance in the face of Nazi aggression. Around him rolling stock has been reduced to matchwood and the roof is now open to the elements. From the look of it the rear of the building had suffered less from the attack. *Mick Webber Collection*

Another three day delay was caused to route 46 trams by a UXB on Eltham Hill. The Luftwaffe seemed to have had it in for Well Hall Roundabout, because the roadway was again blocked by bomb craters on 14th October. Tracks on Eltham Hill were also out of commission. After repairs at Well Hall, cars on routes 44 and 46 were able to reach Eltham Church. An augmented service on bus route 21 was operated from Eltham Church to Lewisham. The rest of the month saw heightened disruption across most of South London.

As an antidote to all the carnage going on, a set of wiring including a turning circle was installed in Villacourt Road, Plumstead. This extension permitted short working vehicles to supply a more extensive service on the Woolwich to Plumstead axis. Residents unhappy about the appearance of trolleybuses running past their select, semi-detached, suburban villas were told they had to accept sacrifices to aid the war effort!

The month of November saw major incidents at Abbey Wood and Bexleyheath depots. Eight trams and twenty-seven trolleybuses received varying degrees of damage to bodywork and electrical equipment. In fact Abbey Wood was hit twice during November, thus obliging the Board to release more former East Ham and West Ham cars from storage in order to fill gaps in the fleet. Another local incident occurred on 8th November, when Woolwich Church Street was rendered impassable for trams. Disruption to routes entering central London was happening on a daily basis. Tracks serving New Cross, Peckham, Old Kent Road, Kennington, Elephant & Castle, Walworth Road and Victoria Embankment were put out of action. Although the term 24/7 was probably unknown at the time, it reflects the availability of emergency crews to repair rails and overhead wires. Many of these brave people risked their lives to keep the show on the road.

Christmas and New Year 1941 brought little respite to the embattled local transport network. On 27th December New Cross Depot received a number of direct hits resulting in the front of the building being completely demolished. Luckily most of the active fleet was out on the road at the time, therefore services to Woolwich, Abbey Wood and Eltham were only marginally affected. The month of January brought a clutch of bomb damage incidents in the New Cross and Greenwich areas. Trams were usually halted at a safe distance from craters in the roadway. Passengers then had to negotiate duck boards and temporary paths to reach a connecting vehicle on the undamaged side of the gap.

On 28th January single line working, using inspectors as human tokens, was instituted on routes 44, 46 and 72, when Grand Depot Road, Woolwich was impassable. Woolwich New Road was used in both directions, until repair crews could complete their work. In order to avoid unnecessary use of the inspectors' time, a convoy system was organised of two or three trams following one another.

In Plumstead by Griffin Road a reversing wye for trolleybuses was wired up and operational from 18th March. This short working facility came in the nick of time, because Plumstead was targeted by the enemy on 19th April. Tram routes 36 and 38, plus trolleybuses 696 and 698, were curtailed. Large craters at Basildon Road and across the junction with Wickham Lane effectively prevented any further progress. A similar situation arose in

Eltham nine days later. Cars on route 46 were unable to proceed past Lee Green in the Woolwich direction. Worse was to follow on 2nd May 1941, when a UXB blocked Eltham Road. Cars on routes 46 and 72 were curtailed at Sidcup Road crossover, whilst vehicles on the 44 worked as far as Yorkshire Grey roundabout. Several 44s were observed running off route along Westhorne Avenue. Emergency buses were called upon from Eltham Church to Sidcup Road via a diversion through the Middle Park Estate.

On 11th/12th May the Luftwaffe attempted to burn down London in one protracted fire raid on the capital. Streets were blocked across the central area; overhead wires were brought down between Woolwich and Abbey Wood. As might be expected, the clear up operation lasted some time and it was only by the middle of June that something like normality was restored. By then the might of the German air force was turned on the Soviet Union, thus effectively ending the blitz on London.

Sporadic raids continued, but they never reached the intensity of the period from September 1940 to May 1941. Thoughts of those in power at 55 Broadway turned to more constructive ways of improving the local transport infrastructure. Unfortunately the actual dates are lacking, but sometime in late 1941/early 1942, an armed soldier accompanied by a couple of individuals with surveying equipment were observed taking measurements and making notes on the Dover Road between Dartford and Gravesend. Information as their presence in the area 'leaked' to George Tapp, the union rep at Bexleyheath Depot. It appeared the LPTB were making plans for the extension of the 696 trolleybus route to Gravesend.

Because of the air of secrecy covering any new transport facility in wartime, George had to be rather circumspect in his inquiries. He contacted his opposite number at Northfleet Bus Garage. Rather predictably, information on the project was very sketchy, but the surveying party had been seen at Northfleet. They had been 'entertained' by the management at the crews' canteen on site. George believed from what he had heard that the forecourt of Northfleet Garage had been measured for the wiring of a possible trolleybus turning circle.

All this presents an intriguing 'what might have been'. The installation of a trolleybus route east of Dartford was quite within the capabilities of the LPTB, which had the resources, both in materials and manpower. Conduits for electrical feeder cables existed as far as Horns Cross and, one presumes, from Galley Hill to the centre of Gravesend. The Board already owned a parcel of land at Horns Cross, which could have been used for a substation. Was there a similar decommissioned building in the Northfleet area, which the BET had constructed? It could have been reactivated.

One extension which did happen involved the construction of overhead wiring from the cramped Woolwich Ferry terminus to a turning circle at Parsons Hill. The new 696 and 698 terminus was inaugurated on 14th July 1943. Trolleybuses now ran from the change pit on Market Hill over a short stretch of road equipped with conduit tram tracks for routes 36, 38 and 40. Later in October of the same year the former battery turn at Princes Road, Crayford was wired for trolleybuses. Heavy peak hour traffic for workers at the nearby Vickers factory necessitated this reversing point.

Woolwich was also the location for a short addition to the tramway network. In Beresford Square a connecting curve was laid from Greens End to Beresford Street, It opened for business on 27th August 1944, and it enabled trams from Eltham to reach factories on the Woolwich Road without reversing in the square. It was used for these special journeys in the morning peak hours. Homeward bound passengers after the day's work did not benefit from any new trackwork. They had to put up with the tram reversing at the first crossover in Plumstead Road!

Although the Blitz was over, the aerial threat remained. It took a more pernicious form, when the enemy perfected 'revenge weapons'. Pilotless V1 flying bombs and V2 rockets were aimed at the south east corner of the country. On 29th June 1944 Bexleyheath Depot received one such unwelcome visit. According to official figures some 84 trolleybuses sustained damage; however, due to swift action by staff, buses and trolleybuses ferried in from other depots managed to cope with the evening rush hour on the day of the incident. Of the vehicular casualties at the depot, twelve were completely destroyed and a further twenty-six trolleybuses were later rebuilt with new bodywork.

Hostilities ended on 8th May 1945. The human cost had been great. At Abbey Wood Depot twenty-two employees had been injured, some seriously; Bexleyheath Depot had suffered one fatality and sixteen members of staff injured. The London Transport roll of honour bears the names of 810 servicemen and 453 civilians, who had lost their lives. This total includes forty-eight tram staff killed on duty and 800, who had been injured.

Like some surrealist painting entitled 'Mangled Trolleybuses' this scene of twisted metal demonstrates the aftermath of an enemy attack in November 1940. Allegedly, the picture features trolleybuses 406 and 795. Incredibly, both vehicles were later rebodied and returned to service. *Mick Webber Collection*

9 Disappearance

The trolleybus had been a popular vehicle in the 1930s. It had a champion in Lord Ashfield, chairman of the LPTB. In the early post war years plans for the completion of the tram conversion programme were dusted off. At first there was nothing to suggest that residents of Sherard Road, Eltham would not have to endure the presence of trolleybus overhead wires. However, the pendulum was swinging in favour of the diesel bus. On 15th November 1946 an official announcement confirmed rumours that the internal combustion engine had triumphed over electric traction. Immediate action was not contemplated. The elimination of London's remaining tramways would have to wait until sufficient resources were available.

The trams were living on borrowed time. They were granted one last hurrah. Route 44 cars, which from the 1910 opening of the line had worked from Woolwich to Eltham Church, were extended on 12th December 1947 to terminate outside the Yorkshire Grey public house in Eltham Road. True to old LCC temperance traditions, the name of the pub never appeared on destination blinds. The terminus at a crossover just a few yards west of the roundabout was designated officially as Middle Park Avenue.

It was now apparent that routes 696 and 698 would remain physically isolated from the rest of the trolleybus network. As such, the proposed extension of the 698 to Eltham would never materialise, nor would Bexleyheath Depot require more space to accommodate extra vehicles. Indeed, doubts were expressed in some quarters as to the continued viability of the trolleybuses, when the original fleet came up for renewal. However, those thoughts were put on hold, because the remaining trams were first in the firing line.

The LPTB ceased to exist on 1st January 1948, to be replaced by the London Transport Executive. To all intents and purposes the dedication of the denizens of 55 Broadway to tramway abandonment remained constant. Few voices were raised against the plans. Officials at London Transport were urged to look at the experience of other continental European cities, which had modernised their tramways. This advice fell on deaf ears. Once the diesel bus fleet had acquired sufficient new vehicles, the melancholy process commenced on 30th September 1950 with routes associated with Wandsworth Depot. The abandonment plan envisaged nine stages, which involved the decommissioning of groups of tram routes. In practice the concluding two stages were combined. Services 36, 38, 40, 44, 46 and 72 were the last to operate.

Penhall Road, Charlton was the final resting place of most London tramcars. Sidings leading off a spur from Woolwich Road connected to a specially constructed scrap yard, where vehicles were unceremoniously burnt. The events of the last day of operation, 5th July 1952, have been chronicled elsewhere; suffice to say, the trams did good business right up to the end.

Although it was not a legal requirement to display L plates for a motorman under instruction, the practice was adopted by London Transport inspectors. Here at the bottom of Beresford Street car 1019 edges round the curve leading to Market Hill. This area was heavily 'blitzed' and there is evidence here of post war reconstruction. Car 1019 ended its life in May 1951 at Penhall Road scrap yard. *Alan Watkins*

E/1 class car 1568 halts at the top of Basildon Road on a frosty winter's morning. Note the separate wiring arrangements for trams and trolleybuses. As can be seen here, the Abbey Wood routes were always well patronised. Some of those boarding the tram will be going to work in the many shops, businesses and light engineering works between Plumstead and Greenwich. Commuting to central London was possible by tram, but it was quicker and more practical to use one of the electrified Southern Region railway lines. *Alan Watkins*

Car 1402 crosses Woolwich Common on about the only rural section of the post war tram system. Sometimes top deck passengers would be treated to the sight of teams from the Royal Artillery guiding horse drawn gun limbers, as they practised in the fields. In common with tramway permanent way workers, the military also employed a scissors crossover. Only theirs was done at speed with two gun limbers missing one another by inches! This line of trees was lost to Dutch elm disease in the late 1960s.

The loss of the rail bound vehicles brought forth a mixed response. Local residents were accustomed to a fixed track transport system, which engendered a feeling of reliability. Trams turned up in all weathers providing a frequent service with cheap fares. Buses lacked the mystique and romance of the vehicles they replaced.

In the months after the last tram week work continued on the reconstruction of New Cross and Abbey Wood depots. Streets were closed and traffic diverted, as outside contractors lifted tram tracks and reinstated road surfaces. Large quantities of Jarrah hard wood blocks and granite setts were dumped in piles on pavements to be removed later by lorries or illicitly by local residents! Beresford Square escaped these highway repairs and tram rails remained visible for many decades. Some traction standards were initially retained for street lighting purposes, but by the mid 1950s Woolwich Borough Council concrete lamp posts had supplanted them.

Overhead wires still existed for the trolleybuses, which continued to operate from the two Woolwich termini at Parsons Hill and North Woolwich Ferry Approach. Amongst the travelling public the habit of going 'to catch the trolley' was ingrained. Passengers liked the smooth ride, the frequent services and the absence of diesel fumes. If the regulars on the 696/698 had been given the choice, the trolleybuses would have lasted a lot longer than they did. Sadly, the powers that be thought otherwise.

68

Your author can testify to the popularity of the trolleys. On a Saturday morning at Welling Corner no sooner had one Dartford bound 696 loaded passengers, than another bus would appear round the corner to mop up folk who hadn't managed to board the first vehicle. A knowledge of rudimentary physics was acquired by any child standing on the staircase, as the trolleybus accelerated away from the bus stop. The juvenile feel of the 'G' forces contrasted with the sluggish experience riding on the average diesel bus.

In March 1951 no fewer than 86 vehicles were allocated to Bexleyheath Depot. Many of them had been rebodied from previously war damaged rolling stock. They weren't the only occupants of the property. Diesel buses on routes 229 and 122 used the forecourt of the depot as a convenient parking space at the end of their journeys.

On 28th April 1954, a public statement from the London Transport Executive announced a £10 million conversion scheme, which aimed to rid the capital of all trolleybuses save for several routes in West London and the Kingston area. Routes 696/698 were to the fore of the abandonment programme. Various ideas were mooted by LTE officials for retiring the 698 in favour of 64 seater Routemaster buses, but delivery problems concerning the latter scuppered the plans. In the end a surplus of the well known RT type diesel buses was pencilled in as a solution to the problem.

In the months before the final abandonment nature took a hand on Friday, 5th September 1958, when a spectacular thunderstorm struck South East England. Extensive flooding, especially in the Welling and Crayford areas, caused damage to vehicles. Six trolleybuses were rescued from the scrap line at Fulwell Depot to be pressed into service at Bexleyheath, while the casualties were dried out. Things did not return to normal for two weeks.

After the demise of the trams, Woolwich and the North Kent towns still benefited from electric street traction in the shape of trolleybus routes 696/698. The terminus at Parsons Hill was pleasantly laid out, but lacked any loop wiring, so that buses could easily pass one another. The alternative for crews was to stow the trolley poles and let others get by. D3 class 519 (DLY 519) heads the queue on a short working to the depot. H1 class 804B (ELB 804), easily recognisable as a rebodied vehicle by the fleet number and the radiused edges to the front upper deck windows, is also making for Bexleyheath but by a different route.

A couple of London's distinctive bowstring bracket traction standards line West Hill, Dartford, as D2 class 451B descends the gradient towards the town centre. The trolleybus has recently passed an RT type green country bus on route 480. Note that the indicator blind on 451B has already been changed for the return trip to Woolwich. *Don Thompson*

Overhead wiring leading to the Springfield Road loop in Welling is depicted above D2 class 410 as it traverses the High Street. Such backstreet turning loops were a feature of the London system; another was situated in Plumstead at Villacourt Road. Note the other road vehicles of predominantly British manufacture and the ease with which parking spaces could be found. *Don Thompson*

Courtleet Parade on the Erith Road is the setting for D2 class 417, pursued by B2 class 98C. The latter may be on a driver training mission from Bexleyheath Depot. In the background is Milestones Garage, which displays the traditional AA, Shell and BP signs. *Don Thompson*

A driver and conductor chat in the spring sunshine next to bowstring standard 252 on Picardy Street, Belvedere. Meanwhile 471 passes on route 698 heading for Abbey Wood. Since this photo was taken in the 1950s, the area has been redeveloped and the road realigned south of this location, behind the advertising hoardings on the right of the picture. *Don Thompson*

A similar outcome for the rest of the local fleet was confirmed by the appearance of yellow conversion notices affixed to traction standards. Routes 696/698 would pass into oblivion on 3rd March 1959. Just after midnight in the wee small hours of 4th March, trolleybus 412B departed Dartford for the depot, thus bringing down the curtain on the electric traction era, which had started with the Gravesend experiment in April 1889.

London Transport seemed very complacent about the possible problems that the changeover to diesel buses would create. In a BBC television interview on the 6.15 evening regional news of 3rd March, the divisional engineer A E Butler in answer to a question: 'Do you think this is going to mean a better service for your passengers?' replied 'Definitely yes' and gave the usual response about the restriction in movement that applied to the trolleybuses. Your author has his own memories soon after the replacement of trolleybus route 696 including the first Saturday of bus operation on the route, now numbered 96 like the tram route the trolleybus had replaced just over 23 years earlier. A 'better service' it was certainly not and unheard of waits at bus stops were common. The main reason for this was a savage reduction in capacity on the route when 56 seater RTs took over from the 70 seater trolleybuses. Not only did the buses have fewer seats there were also fewer vehicles: a maximum schedule of 36 RTs compared to 51 trolleybuses. This was a total capacity reduction of over 42%. This was compensated to a small degree by other route changes, but the new schedules were clearly inadequate. People wanted the trolleybuses back; a futile hope. One wonders how many folk stuck in queues that Saturday morning decided they would bite the bullet, take out hire purchase and buy a car!

During the rest of March and into April of 1959 overhead wires were cut down. Traction standards were uprooted except when required by the local authorities as street lamps. At least one of these former trolleybus poles, painted in Bexley LB blue, survived into the late 1970s at Bexleyheath Clock Tower. Almost nothing now remains to remind the casual observer of a past era of environmentally friendly public transport.

At the time of writing, Bexleyheath Depot (now bus garage) still stands; however, Abbey Wood, Erith and Bexley tram depots have long since disappeared. One remarkable relic of the past is the Old Tramyard, Lakedale Road, Plumstead, which was the site of the WSELT depot and later a temporary car shed for the LCC. In Woolwich New Road the Tramshed Theatre now occupies the original sub station building constructed by the LCC. In Beresford Square, after surviving for many years, the preserved tram track layout complete with granite setts was sacrificed to an act of civic vandalism, when the whole lot was resurfaced.

We are left with the memories of the sound of tramcars climbing Well Hall Road, Eltham or the sight of a seemingly endless procession of trolleybuses travelling along Bexleyheath Broadway or turning by the Clock Tower.

The imposition of diesel buses in place of electric traction contributed in no small measure to heightened levels of urban pollution. Unfortunately, critics of these decisions remained unheard in the 1950s and 1960s. In the face of global climate change the abandonment of trams and trolleybuses now appears totally ill advised.

D2 class 444 makes the turn at Bexleyheath Clock Tower. Here on the Broadway was a great place to go trolleybus watching, due to the endless stream of vehicles arriving and departing. The chap on the back platform better hold tight as he ascends the stairs. Trolleybuses were well known for their instant acceleration from a standing start. *C.Carter*

Time is running out for the trolleybuses. In this superbly atmospheric photo taken in Erith at dusk, D2 class 470B is working short to Plumstead Station. Your author cannot recall speaking to anyone at the time of conversion in March 1959, who wanted the local pattern of transport disrupted by diesel buses. In fact the opposite was true and folk resented being deprived of 'their' trolleys by those in power at 55 Broadway, SW1. *Alan Cross*

10 Infrastructure

Horse Tramway Depots

One of the requirements of horse tramway operation was the construction of a depot yard encompassing car sheds and stables. Here the fleet could be kept securely and the equine motive power could be supervised professionally by veterinary trained personnel.

In an article written in 1900 an eyewitness describes the scene:

It is 8 am and at the entrance to a big London tramyard stand some eight or nine smartly uniformed conductors and leather aproned drivers. Close by, in the yard inspector's office are three conductors receiving their boxes of tickets and signing for them in a big many columned book. A car comes slowly from the back of the yard; a conductor jumps on, dons his bell punch and prepares for work.

The London County Council cars, filled with almost every type of the great city's male and female workers, are following each other closely on their way to the termini at Southwark, Blackfriars, Waterloo and Westminster Bridge. During the afternoon the trams in all parts are less crowded, but at 6 pm they begin to fill up rapidly at every terminus.

At ten o'clock the trams begin to pass into the yards. At long intervals at first, but after eleven o'clock every two or three minutes. A horse drawn tram, its last journey for the day ended, enters the yard. A stableman is there awaiting it, and the moment it stops, he promptly takes out the horses and leads them upstairs to unharness, feed and make them secure for the night.

The driver then marches off home with his rug on his arm and his whip in his hand. The conductor, however, is not quite ready to depart; for two or three minutes he sits inside the car checking his last journey's takings. Having made his money agree with his waybill, he enters the little yard office and hands it in, together with his unused tickets, to the night inspector.

When the last tram has entered the yard, which is now crowded with cars, the gates are shut and the washers and stablemen are left to themselves. The washers vigorously sweep the dirt and the discarded tickets from the roofs and insides of the cars. Not until this task is ended, is the washing begun. It is nearly 5am before the last car is washed, but the washers work is not yet finished. The windows have to be cleaned, the brass work polished and the panels rubbed with chamois leather.

This account of life at a London horse tram depot confirms how labour intensive it all was. There were always many men available to fill any jobs on offer. Although the LCC was acknowledged as a good employer, all members of staff lived with the fear that even a minor infraction of the rules could cost an individual his livelihood. Hours were long and dealing with the travelling public was no sinecure.

Vehicles belonging to the standard gauge Pimlico, Peckham and Greenwich Company were accommodated from 1871 in a car shed and stables in Greenwich Road. Later in 1894 another set of buildings was erected at the northern end of Lower Park Street, Greenwich. In the first decade of the twentieth century this depot was pulled down and the site used for the new LCC power station.

The WSELT operated out of a depot in Plumstead at Lakedale Road. In the late spring of 1881 this was ready to house 41 horses, plus six tramcars with knifeboard seating on the top deck. As with many metropolitan operators, the Woolwich company was always 'well horsed' in contrast to some of the more impecunious provincial tramways. Although buses and trams competed for custom on certain routes, companies such as the London General Omnibus and Tillings negotiated hiring agreements for the supply of horses to several London tramway undertakings.

During the electrification period after acquisition by the LCC, various temporary expedients for the accommodation of the former WSELT fleet included a depot on Tunnel Avenue. This facility required the laying of 200 yards of connecting track to the main route on Woolwich Road. Economy was the watchword; cars stood in the open with tarpaulins over the top decks; horses fared better under cover in a small galvanised iron building.

On the electrified section from Beresford Street to Plumstead the former WSELT premises at Lakedale Road was equipped with dual gauge tracks so that, pending the inauguration of Abbey Wood Depot, electric trams could share the site with horsecars. The latter were conveyed to and from the remaining short section of horse tramway between Chapel Street and Nile Street on a four wheel, standard gauge trolley fitted with a ramp and narrow gauge rails. This unusual arrangement functioned well until one morning in November 1911, when the horses attached to the trolley bolted and were seriously injured by impact with a plate glass window in the Mitre Pub.

The Gravesend, Rosherville & Northfleet Tramways Company depot was on the west side of The Hill, Northfleet. Three narrow gauge tracks led to a car shed with a corrugated iron extension for the two experimental electric vehicles. It was closed in 1901 and demolished to make way for a church.

Electric Tramway Depots

The <u>Abbey Wood Car Shed</u> was situated a couple of hundred yards from the terminus at Knee Hill, which straddled the county boundary. Costed at £10,644 for the building, plus £3,675 for the electrical infrastructure including overhead wiring, the depot was ready by February 1910. Unlike some other LCC car sheds, the architecture was a very plain style of 'tramway vernacular'. An office block was also constructed next to the entrance with a frontage on Abbey Wood Road.

An extension was opened in October 1914. The building featured a traverser giving access to twenty stabling roads. In theory a total of 86 tramcars could be housed here, but in practice this figure was never reached. The track layout outside incorporated a reversing triangle, so that trailers could be shunted more efficiently.

After the Eltham to Lee Green tracks were connected, Abbey Wood began a settled period of supplying vehicles for services 36, 38 and 46 in cooperation with New Cross Depot. Trams for weekday route 44 were also based at Abbey Wood. This routine continued after acquisition by the LPTB in July 1933, until the closure of Erith Depot on 28th December 1933, when cars working what was to become service 98 came into the fold. The latter disappeared after the opening of Bexleyheath Trolleybus Depot on 10th November 1935.

Plans were drawn up in conjunction with the Board's South London trolleybus proposals. These envisaged a separate eastern exit to the modified depot, which was calculated to have a capacity of 60 trolleybuses. When the policy changed after the war, the plans were dusted off and altered for conversion to diesel buses. Temporary tracks were laid on the concrete floor required for the transformation into a bus garage. Retention of the tramway traversers was imperative, until the last night of the London system on 5th July 1952. With the rail bound inmates evicted, it took some months to remove rails and traverser, in order to make the building fully functional for the replacing buses. The cost of the whole garage renovation was £165,000.

Although not part of our main story, the fate of AW garage, as it was coded by London Transport, was determined on 30th October 1981, when it was replaced by the new Plumstead (PD) Garage. The building has subsequently been demolished.

On 28th June 1952 photographer Alan Cross visited Abbey Wood Depot, then in the throes of conversion to a bus garage. The hand written sign is self explanatory. Less obvious is the reason for the presence of the barrel organ. One assumes it wasn't left by mistake on one of the trams. Ex West Ham car 307 looks marooned amidst the scaffolding and concrete mixers. As it is a Saturday afternoon, it is likely that everyone concerned with the rebuilding work has knocked off for the weekend. *Alan Cross*

The Erith UDC Tram Depot was sited adjacent to the attractively named Walnut Tree Road, a thoroughfare constructed new for the tramways. The building had four roads with a capacity of sixteen trams; later this became nineteen plus a works car. The site also contained offices, workshops, basic facilities for the staff and a maintenance store. Part of the depot was occupied by a paint shop, which maintained the appearance of the apple green and primrose liveried fleet.

Unfortunately, due to the impoverished state of the Erith undertaking, the depot building was neglected and had deteriorated by the early 1930s, so that many of the pleasant architectural features on the façade had vanished under a layer of grime.

The end came on 28th December 1933, when the LPTB moved vehicles to Abbey Wood Depot. The site was then used by the Board as a store, but was offered back to Erith Council, who took full possession in March 1935. Ironically, the depot outlived the trolleybus era and was still substantially intact in the early 1970s. Your author was a member of an organised visit to the depot in 1975 and can testify to the fact that it was easy to imagine the interior full of trams again. Track was still in place; the roof troughs plus vestiges of the overhead wiring could be clearly seen.

The depot was worth preserving, but there were more pressing needs for local regeneration and the area was flattened in 1978.

The Erith Depot building is depicted shortly after the takeover by the LPTB in July 1933. A mixed fleet of covered top and open top vehicles are available for service, but they are living on borrowed time. Most of the old rolling stock would shortly be moved out by the new owners. *Alan Cross*

The <u>Bexley UDC Tram Depot</u> was situated on the south side of Bexleyheath Broadway between the Clock Tower and Gravel Hill. In the depot yard a track fan lead to six stabling roads, each approached by an arched entrance. The rails inside the building were supported on brick piers, thus enabling maintenance staff to move beneath vehicles in order to effect repairs. The building originally had a capacity of 18 cars, but latterly after the Dartford fire disaster the site became home to 34 tramcars.

The depot was surveyed in preparation for the LPTB takeover in July 1933. It was initially thought that both this site and its companion in Erith were unsuitable for further tramway operation. Consultations with the former owners, Bexley UDC, resulted in a change of heart and cancellation of plans to place temporary tracks in what was to become Bexleyheath Trolleybus Depot.

Closure came on 23rd November 1935 with the inmates being driven away to a new home at West Ham Depot. The local authority then regained possession of the area, which outlived the trolleybuses running on route 696. Residents of a certain age would refer to the place as 'the old depot, where they used to keep the flying bedsteads that rocked and swayed all over the place and sometimes left the track!' The building attained minor celebrity status and a number of people actually expressed regret, when the structure was demolished in the 1970s.

Pictured in the first few months after acquisition by the LPTB, an ex LCC works car stands on the depot track fan at Bexley. This vehicle has probably has its work cut out in an attempt to bring the local tram tracks up to standard. The cable drum and sundry other building materials indicate the site was being used as a storage facility, pending the opening of Bexleyheath Trolleybus Depot.

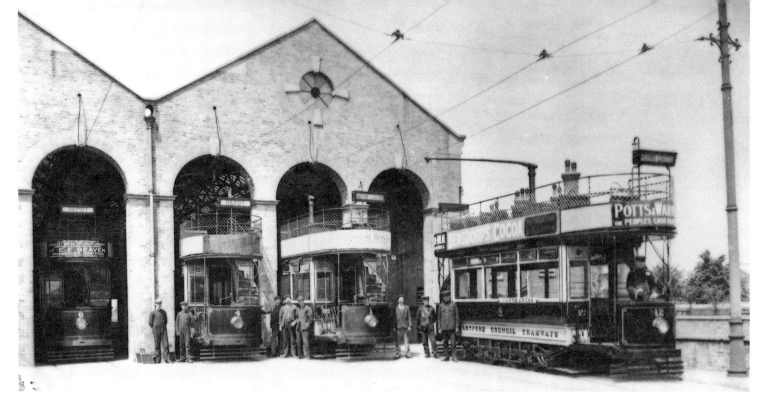

Cars 6, 4, 1 and 12 stand in the sunshine outside the depot in Victoria Road. The plain, but attractive frontage of the tram shed had echoes of the building serving the Bexley system with brick arches topping each entry road. As is mentioned in the text, this whole area was destroyed by fire in August 1917.

The Dartford UDC Tram Depot was constructed in Burnham Road at the end of the branch serving Victoria Road, Dartford Station and Hythe Street. Brick built in a very utilitarian style, the depot frontage included a yard with a track fan leading to four storage roads. The building had a capacity of 16 tramcars; the ex Erith demi car was subsequently added to the fleet.

As is well known, the complete structure and the tramcars contained within perished in a devastating fire in August 1917. The conflagration was so fierce that nothing could be salvaged from the ruins. Certainly there was no time for any of the rolling stock to be rescued. Damage was estimated at £17,000 and the cause was said to be a cigarette butt left on one of the cars by a passenger, who was part of the August Bank Holiday crowds.

The site was later levelled, although certain ancillary buildings such as the power station survived. In the 1920s and 1930s eyewitness reports confirm that the track on Hythe Street was retained for short workings to Dartford Station. Overhead wires continued to the power station, which still supplied power to the network.

The Gravesend & Northfleet Electric Tramways Company Depot with a capacity of 20 trams was constructed on a vacant plot near the Dover Road tramway; its northern boundary lay adjacent to the SER North Kent main line. Unusually, the approach tracks in the depot yard were not paved, but ballasted railway fashion. Five storage tracks, each with inspection pits, entered the building, which was constructed of brick to a very plain design. The British Electric Traction Company, owners of the Gravesend setup, favoured this approach rather than the more expensive, ornate styles, which mirrored municipal pride and were beloved of local councils.

After the demise of the trams, the site was used for motor buses and it subsequently passed into the ownership of the LPTB, who used the premises until the opening of Northfleet Garage in 1937. At the time of writing (2020) much of the original building is still in existence.

Trolleybus Infrastructure

It was a British linguistic tradition that trams and trolleybuses were housed in depots, but diesel buses inhabited garages. The LPTB adhered to this custom. In fact, trolleybuses were regarded legally as trackless trams; working practices for crews and staff resembled those of the former tramways and were in many respects dissimilar to those found in the central red bus department administered by 55 Broadway. This distinction ceased in May 1962 with the abandonment of electric traction in London.

Another British institution was the depot cat. This particular feline was expected to earn its keep by terrorising the rodent population. Animal lovers amongst the crews at both Erith and Bexley tram depots maintained the tradition after transferring to trolleybuses. As an honorary member of the Transport & General Workers Union, the Bexleyheath 'moggie' was a valued member of staff.

Because of the unsuitability of the two tram depots at Erith, Walnut Tree Road and at Bexleyheath Broadway, a completely new facility to a modern (1930s) design was constructed by the LPTB opposite Pelham Road on the eastern side of Erith Road. Situated on route 698, the building lay a few yards within the jurisdiction of Crayford UDC. The layout featured a through flow for trolleybuses, instead of the turntable/traverser arrangement normally associated with converted tram depots. A complete circle of overhead wiring surrounded the depot. This was used for driver training and (wholly unofficially) for contestants in a fastest lap competition. The spacious forecourt provided a convenient terminal stand for diesel buses on routes 122 and 229. Capacity under cover was 75 trolleybuses of Leyland manufacture. The depot was coded BX by London Transport.

There is plenty happening in this late 1950s view of Bexleyheath Trolleybus Depot. Employees' cars occupy a space to the right of the picture, while at the other end of the depot a couple of RT type buses await their turn to depart on central bus routes 122 and 229. Note the traction standards protected by a concrete collar at the base. *C.Carter*

D2 class 430 (DGY 430) pulls over to pick up a passenger on the railway bridge over the Southern Electric line from Woolwich to Dartford. Note the intricacies of the overhead wiring, whereby none of the traction standards were actually positioned on the structure of the bridge. *N.Rayfield*

Since inauguration in November 1935 the internal wiring layout was altered several times. A repair shop included docking pits, a paint shop and stores. Accommodation was also provided for breakdown vehicles and a tower wagon. On the south side of the building there were traffic offices, an oil store and a shed for employees' bicycles. In the mid 1940s there were plans to enlarge the depot. It is thought this was in anticipation of the extension of route 698 to Eltham, which failed to materialise. During the war the depot was badly damaged and was rebuilt to basically original condition.

Traction standards with white painted concrete collars at their bases were a feature of the forecourt. Several portable 'dolly' stops bore the legend KEEP UNDER WIRE to remind drivers to remain attached to their power source. During the long bus strike of spring 1958 your author, then a schoolboy, observed pickets at the depot, who had altered several of these to read KEEP ON STRIKE!

Also in the same year as the strike, work began on converting the establishment to BX bus garage. On 4th March 1959, a grand total of 61 newly overhauled RT type buses took up service from this location. Over the next few days the condemned trolleybuses were towed away to the scrap yard. Traction standards, overhead wires and associated electrical fittings were removed. The building still exists today.

Track

The laying of rails in public highways was regulated by the Tramways Act of 1870. Even after the local authority and sundry private objectors had been satisfied, the official inspection by the Board of Trade could still unearth issues of concern. Poor paving and unsuitable track layouts were often subject to scrutiny, before permission was granted for the carrying of fare paying passengers. Once these hurdles had been overcome, the business of offering a reliable, daily service began in earnest.

The ideal for any tramway situated in populous areas was to provide double track along the principal thoroughfares. The alternative of single track and passing loops inevitably restricted the nature of the service, when one vehicle had to wait for an oncoming tram before occupying the line ahead. Unlike their railway colleagues, horse tram drivers were normally not subject to the dictates of signals to obtain the right of way.

Electric trams weighed more and operated at higher speeds than their equine antecedents. Consequently they required a substantial track base with heavier rails. The London County Council adopted high standards with well maintained track and paving. It was normal for the LCC to construct routes as double track; however, in the Woolwich are, and in particular on the line to Plumstead and Abbey Wood, narrow streets obliged the council to lay single track and passing loops. Road widening, allowed under the auspices of wartime emergency legislation, cured many of these bottlenecks. Double track speeded up the service for munitions workers to and from the Royal Arsenal.

In the area under review tramway operators plumped for different manufacturers of permanent way materials. Erith used No.3 British Standard girder rails, 60 ft long and weighing 100 pounds per yard; special pointwork was manufactured by Hadfields of Sheffield. Paving included Norwegian granite setts, with Jarrah hardwood blocks outside places of worship. These were used to deaden traffic noise. In contrast to its neighbour, Bexley put faith in Belgian 90 pound rails. Both operators, aside from the Erith town centre to Abbey Wood route, relied on a traditional single line and loops formation, favoured by many of the smaller British tram systems. Dartford and Gravesend also adopted this layout, which relied on line of sight from tram drivers to avoid potentially dangerous meetings with other tramcars on single track.

Point blades on loops were usually sprung in a facing direction, so that trams veered to the left. On double track trailing crossovers the wheels of cars going straight ahead would push the point blade over. This particular facet of operation has survived to the present day and can still be observed on the second generation of UK tramways. Motormen were supplied with a point iron to tackle facing crossovers, such as existed outside Eltham Church, where cars on route 44 had to take the right hand track before they reversed.

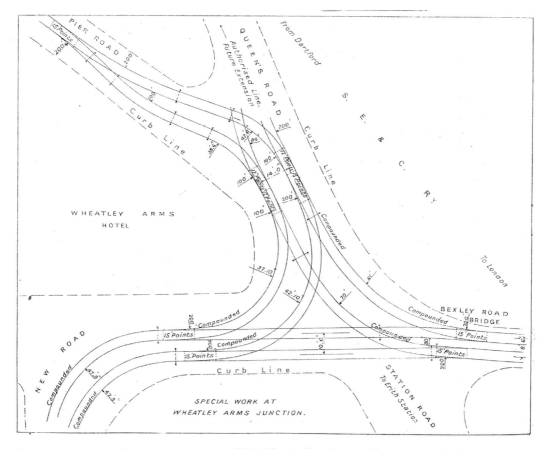

Original permanent way department track layout at Erith, Wheatley Hotel junction. Note the points leading to the proposed branch along Queens Road.

Relaying of track was dependent on finances. There is plenty of evidence to suggest that Bexley and Erith relied heavily on essential welding repairs to keep rolling stock from derailing. They did purchase secondhand rails, but this was only putting off the inevitable. By the time the LPTB came along, most of the track was time expired, thus obliging the Board to issue instructions to motormen of class M vehicles to run at half speed and no faster.

Almost sixty trams an hour used the trackwork on the roundabout outside the Odeon Cinema, Well Hall. Hence the pointwork took a particular pounding. The facing points in the foreground are of the two blade variety, controlled by point motors. This automatic facility required continuous maintenance. Unfortunately in the last few months of the London system, several sets of automatic points here and at the Yorkshire Grey roundabout failed. Motorman then had to rely on the tried and trusted point iron. *Alan Watkins*

Overhead Wiring

In most of the LCC area the alleged problems of unsightly overhead wiring did not arise. The capital adopted the expensive conduit method of conveying electrical power to tramcars. The tried and tested overhead wire and trolley pole current collection system was good enough for everyone else. Even the LCC swallowed its principles and avoided the conduit for its suburban lines.

The Woolwich to Eltham route of the LCC was equipped with double trolley wires; each member of class M operating locally was fitted with two trolley poles. These vehicles possessed switching arrangements, so that they could operate with a single trolley, when negotiating the overhead from Beresford Square to Abbey Wood. After the Eltham section was connected to conduit tracks at Lee Green, a change pit was constructed at the latter location outside the fire station. Double trolley wires then led along Eltham Road, past Eltham Green and along Eltham Hill to meet existing wiring at St John's Church, Eltham High Street.

New through service 46 was worked by E/1 class cars 1366-1400, which were equipped with double trolley poles and were fitted with an electrical device, which could be switched to either conduit, single trolley or double trolley power supply. Tramway motormen and conductors all received technical training, so that they could attempt to rectify any faults their tramcar might suffer 'on the road'.

On 13th November 1927, the twin wire system was replaced by the conventional single wire. Although the second wire was removed in stages, the additional insulators on span wires were left in place; these remained a unique feature of the Eltham routes, until the trams ceased in July 1952.

Both trams and trolleybuses did occasionally suffer dewirements. In which case it was normally up to the conductor to retrieve the errant trolley pole(s). Car 578 is depot bound to Abbey Wood, but the trolley is heading off in the Eltham direction! Luckily, the conductor has spotted the danger.

Although some folk regarded overhead wires as visually intrusive, others liked the patterns of a web of trolley wires. Here at the corner of West Street and Lower Road, Erith, span wires and associated bridling keep the overhead taut. A typical London feature was the string of 'fairy' lights in the middle of the picture. These were illuminated in bad visibility, often during the infamous fogs and smogs of 1940s and 1950s, to guide trolleybus drivers.

Artistic taste in the Edwardian era dictated that traction standards, which were basically spun steel tubes, were decorated with wrought iron work. Metal bases of these tramway poles were made of cast iron, stamped with the coat of arms of the operator. As is well known, the BET adopted a wheel and magnet device, which also appeared on the waist or rocker panels of the company's vehicles. The overhead running wire was suspended from span wires attached to traction standards placed on pavements. The LCC favoured this arrangement rather than employing single poles with bracket arms, as used extensively in Bexley, Erith, Dartford and Gravesend.

In Erith the overhead wires were supplied by Brush of Loughborough at a height of 25 ft above the roadway. Double trolley wire, one for each direction, was employed and was of 3/0 SWG diameter, energised at a pressure of 550 volts DC. Standards with bracket arms 31 ft high could minimise the visual impact of overhead wires by keeping them towards one side of the highway. This method worked well with trams equipped with swivel head trolleys, which could deviate laterally.

Unlike its North Kent neighbours the initial fleet delivered to Gravesend was fitted with fixed head trolleys. These required overhead wires to be placed centrally above the rails. Traction standards with span wires attached were placed opposite one another on either side of the road. Latterly, Gravesend trams employed the usual swivel trolley head system.

Conversion to trolleybuses in 1935 required almost wholesale renewal of wiring and electrical supply networks. New traction standards were planted by the LPTB to replace the old tramway poles, which were uprooted and carted away for scrap. An excellent article explaining the technical aspects of London overhead wiring appeared in *The Transport World* for 14th March 1940, and is reproduced for readers.

Overhead Construction

PRACTICAL EXPERIENCE OF LONDON TRANSPORT

By F. H. WIGNER, A.M.I.E.E., *Overhead Engineer, London Passenger Transport Board*

When the London Passenger Transport Board was formed in 1933, it included in its area 17¼ miles of trolleybus route previously operated by the London United Tramways. The experience gained in this suburban area justified the extension of the trolleybus system, and the Board decided to convert a further 40 route miles where heavy expenditure on track would be necessary if the trams were to continue running. Prior to the conversion of these routes considerable investigation and experiments were carried out and the results embodied in the new construction. Further improvements were made as the work progressed, and the success which attended these initial change-overs led to the Board's decision to convert the remainder of its 327 route miles of tramways to trolleybus operation.

It was realized very early that considerable improvement in the usual standard of overhead construction and current collection would be necessary to satisfy the exacting conditions of the Central London area. To this end records of all delays to service were carefully tabulated and analysed with a view to eliminating all sources of weakness and improving operation.

Shoe Operation

The trolley wheels were considered a source of objectionable noise, and the area of contact with the

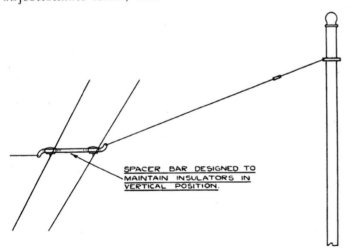

Fig. 1. **Type of Rigid Suspension** ensuring that ears hang vertically

overhead conductor too small to carry the heavy current taken, especially when accelerating.

Early experiments showed the possible advantages of a shoe collector in place of the trolley wheel, and various materials and types of shoes were tried until finally a bronze shoe with a carbon block insert was adopted as standard.

The fittings originally used on the overhead line were those which had been developed for use with the tram with its slower speed and fixed track, and it was

proved that a large proportion of the troubles and delays experienced was due to their use.

Suspension

To ensure smooth running and absence of dewirements at high speeds it is essential to suspend the overhead wire so that the ears hang vertically.

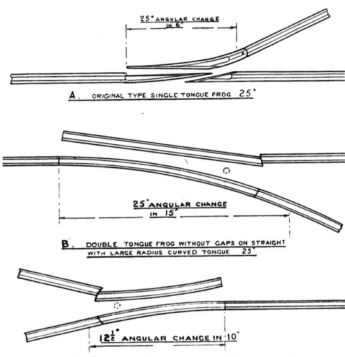

Fig. 2. Below is a double tongue Y frog with large radius curved tongues 25°

Various means have been adopted to meet this requirement, including double span construction, but the Board's engineers have developed a fitting with a rigid steel bar between porcelain insulated wire supports which, when properly erected, holds the ears in an approximately vertical position both on the straight and on curves. (See Fig. 1.) This fitting has proved very satisfactory, and by eliminating the use of the auxiliary span, permits the use of 31 ft. poles under normal conditions.

Frogs

Frogs which had proved satisfactory in tramway practice were found to be unsuitable for trolleybuses, owing to the latter's greater speed, more rapid acceleration, and its varying position relative to the overhead conductors. To overcome this difficulty it was considered necessary to reduce the angular rate of change of direction of the trolley head and also to provide a continuous guide for the shoe in either direction. This was achieved by designing a double-tongued frog with a curved tongue of long radius, the curvature continuing along the fixed part of the branch line. (See Fig. 2.)

A simple locking device was embodied in the design

to prevent any movement of the tongue by pressure of the shoe from side running.

The hand operation of frogs which required the conductor to hold over the frog while the bus passed through and then to run after it, caused delay and a certain element of danger. To remove these objections electrical operation of frogs was decided upon. The usual form of this apparatus actuated by the position of the controller on the vehicle was found to be un-

(1) Freedom from tendency to track under effect of weather and arching from shoes passing over the runner.

(2) Resistance to wear due to friction of shoe.

(3) Resistance to burning from the arcs at break.

(4) No tendency to absorb moisture.

(5) No tendency to deform under the influence of weather conditions.

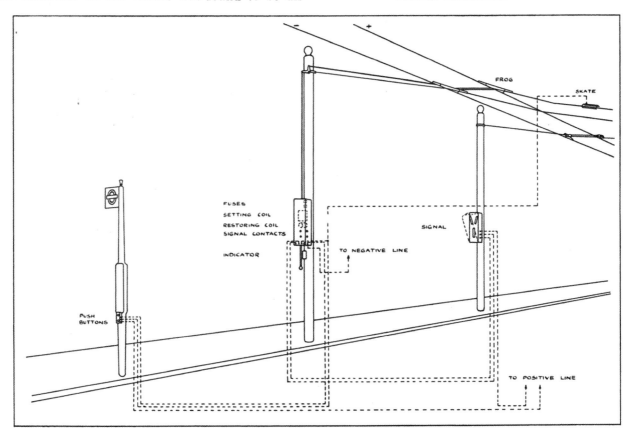

Fig. 3. Wiring Diagram of London Transport Push Button Operated Frogs, Showing Entire Equipment in Use

suitable for use in dense traffic with controlled junctions and also on gradients, and a system was developed for operation of frogs by push buttons.

The push buttons situated on a post or pole at the stopping place close to the frog are operated by the conductor. The position of the frog is shown by an illuminated signal visible to the driver. (See Fig. 3.) The frog having been set by the push button remains in that position until reset either by a contact skate on the overhead wire or by the operation of another button, according to circumstances. This system has proved very effective in practice.

Crossings

Owing to the side pull which tends to twist the shoe at the centre diamond on a fixed crossing and so cause it to dewire or take the wrong direction, it has not been found practicable to design a completely reliable crossing for trolleybuses under 25 deg., although this angle is too wide in many cases.

An experiment which is proving quite successful is the use of crossings with movable tongues, enabling crossings and frogs of 15 deg. to be used in places where a small angle is an advantage.

Insulated Runners

The material now used for insulated runners has been chosen after many tests and trials. The features which an ideal material should possess are :—

While the perfect material has not yet been discovered, difficulties in this respect are no longer serious.

Section Insulators and Insulators at Special Work

The insulators generally used for this purpose in the first sections constructed by the Board have wooden beams for the insulating material. These, largely on account of their unwieldy appearance overhead, and also because of their unreliability mechanically, were not accepted as satisfactory. By co-operation between the Board's engineers and the manufacturers an insulator was developed in which insulated steel rods replaced the wooden beams. This is now employed on the Board's new construction work, and its use has resulted in improved appearance and mechanical reliability of special work construction.

It has been the practice from the time carbon insert shoes were introduced to design the special work to make contact with the metal sides of the shoe and not with the carbon insert. This enables more robust insulated runners to be used and reduces risk of damage to the carbon. The change of contact area is made by forming a ramp at the entering and leaving ends of the special work.

Feeder Pillars

The feeder pillars through which supply is given to the overhead line have been re-designed to comply with modern ideas of appearance, one being of a very compact type for use where space is limited and where other conditions permit.

The power supply is generally from automatically controlled mercury arc rectifier sub-stations. Each automatic circuit breaker in the sub-station can be opened or closed by push buttons in the feeder pillar at either end of the section of overhead wire which it feeds. If current is automatically cut off it is possible for the traffic operation staff to restore it when the fault is clear by operating the " close " button in the feeder pillar. To ensure safety for linesmen when working on the overhead line a clip is provided with the " open " button enabling it to be held in. This prevents current being put on by the operation of the " close " button.

An interesting development has been the negotiations with the London Fire Brigade to provide them with

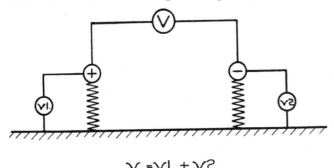

$$V = V1 + V2$$

Fig. 4. Wiring for Testing Insulation of System

means for making the overhead wires dead in emergency. A short-circuiting device and rubber guards have been designed by the Board's engineers to meet the requirements of the Fire Brigade, and facilities for demonstrating this to those concerned in its use have been provided.

The D.C. supply to the overhead wires is wherever practicable given with no permanent " earth " connected either to the positive or negative pole. This has been adopted and investigation has confirmed that the danger of severe shock if contact is made with a live conductor is much less on such a system than on one with one pole permanently earthed. Special means are used for testing the insulation of the system at frequent intervals. (See Fig. 4.)

This test is based on line volts being assumed constant, and readings on a voltmeter taken successively between each pole and " earth " being added together in the instrument itself. A scale on the instruments gives the insulation of the line to " earth " in ohms.

The insulation resistance of the system $R = r\dfrac{(V-1)}{v}$

where r is the resistance of the voltmeter used, V is the supply voltage, and v is the sum of the readings taken between each pole and earth. It can be seen that if V is taken as constant the only variables are the two readings to earth.

Construction

Preliminary plans for the construction showing position of overhead work are drawn after a survey of the routes has been made, during which suitable positions for poles are selected. After the poles have been planted revised plans are prepared and at special work, curves, etc., the lengths of all spans, pull-offs and bridles are indicated, and this greatly speeds up and facilitates construction.

Pole Planting

For pole planting, lorries are used which are equipped with an hydraulic crane operated from the engine of the lorry and controlled by the driver. The advantages of using such a lorry for the purpose are considerable. As it is equipped with a crane the lorry can be taken to the pole dump, the poles picked up, conveyed to site and lowered into the holes prepared for them, thus reducing handling to a minimum. The lorry is used for other purposes, for instance, the crane can pick up and unload a jointer's truck or small drums of cable.

In planting the poles it is often necessary to clear underground obstructions, and for this various methods have been adopted, including :—

(1) Actual bending of the pole.
(2) Offsetting the pole by cutting the pole and fitting into bayonet sockets.
(3) Offsetting the pole by cutting and welding.

The latter is the most modern and in many ways the best for meeting the problem.

The poles used in London are the B.S.I. standard tubular steel poles of the sectional type. Concrete poles have been tried, but in spite of certain advantages they have had to be abandoned in view of their greater bulk and weight for the same strength, and the practical impossibility of adapting them to cope with the obstructions referred to in the previous paragraph.

For the erection of the overhead wire a special trailer has been designed provided with a hand brake on the wire drum and a further brake on a dynamometer wheel around which the wire passes when being run out. With this machine wire can be easily and quickly run out without kinking or undue bending of the wire.

For Maintenance of Overhead Work

Petrol-driven tower wagons with power-operated towers are used for inspection and maintenance of the overhead line. To avoid jerky movement and facilitate slow motion during inspections these vehicles have fluid flywheel transmission. The lorries referred to previously in connection with pole planting are also used for general maintenance work. Great saving in labour on maintenance results from the crane attachment on these lorries.

Lubrication of the wire has been found by experience to be essential, as it not only increases the life of the carbon inserts in the shoes, but reduces the wear on the overhead wire and prevents any noise arising from the current collector. A graphite lubricating varnish made in the Board's laboratories is applied to the overhead wire by special petrol-driven vehicles. The varnish is applied to the wire by means of a wheel running in a small tank attached to a boom. This fluid dries on the wire in a few seconds. The vehicle can apply this when running at 10 M.P.H. It is found that good results are obtained if the wire is lubricated every 8,000 passes, or once every two weeks where services are less dense.

The life of the trolley wire has been greatly increased by the adoption of shoes with carbon inserts and by the lubrication of the wire. Even on heavy routes and under ears on up gradients the wear of wire is so small that no accurate estimate of its life can yet be given ; it may well be that fatigue will finally be the determining factor.

Appendices

1. Joyce Green Hospital Tramway

In the late 1890s the Metropolitan Asylums Board constructed three isolation hospitals on the banks of the Thames. Joyce Green, situated north of Dartford town centre was the largest of the group. A causeway connected Orchard Hospital, adjacent to Joyce Green, with Long Reach Hospital, which possessed a landing stage on the River Thames. Internal transport for patients and staff was provided by a network of horse worked tramways of 4 feet/1219mm gauge. Single deck cars were fitted out with beds and stretcher carriers.

As one of the last operating horse tramways in Britain, equine motive power was finally retired in 1925 to be replaced by Talbot motor ambulances, which towed the tramcars, either singularly or in trains of two vehicles coupled together. Operation ceased in the mid 1930s and track was lifted for the wartime scrap metal drive. Vestiges of the permanent way still existed at the Joyce Green site in 1970; however, the whole area has since been redeveloped.

What is otherwise a standard 1870s horsecar is remarkable for the experimental running gear. A six wheel radial version has been substituted for the conventional rigid four wheel, single truck. Engineer to the Greenwich Company was J.D.Larsen, who had produced a similar vehicle for the Paris Exhibition of 1878. Sadly, we do not know whether this revolutionary tramcar actually took to the rails in South East London.

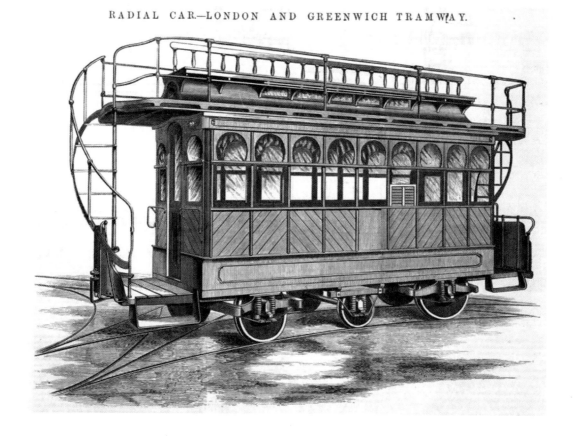

RADIAL CAR.—LONDON AND GREENWICH TRAMWAY.

2. Rolling Stock

Horse Trams

Early vehicles of the Pimlico, Peckham & Greenwich Street Tramways Company were built by Drew & Burnett of Fountainbridge (Edinburgh). Weight of the cars was between 2 tons 5 cwt (2.26 tonnes) and 2 tons 7 cwt (2.38 tonnes). The exact size of the fleet is unknown, but there were at least nine vehicles of the double deck type, which resembled the original Starbuck cars of 1861-2.

We are on safer ground, when sorting out the rolling stock of the Woolwich undertaking. On the LCC takeover a total of thirty-two cars were recorded, of which seventeen were normally used in service. The motive power consisted of 200 horses. By the time the WSELT was incorporated into the LCC a number of the original horse tramcars had been scrapped following accident damage.

Six double deck cars with five window lower saloons, built by the Metropolitan Railway Carriage & Wagon Company, at a cost of £165 each, formed the initial fleet. These were followed in 1882 by another six vehicles from the same manufacturer. They were slightly larger with a six window lower saloon. Purchase price was £212. In 1884 ten similar cars were acquired at a cost of £221 each.

This scene features Gravesend car 2 near the Leather Bottel, Northfleet. These two horse, double deckers accommodated 18 inside and 22 on transverse garden seats, fixed to the top deck. Allegedly, this view was taken on the visit of the directors of the company. Two members of the depot staff look after the horses to the right of the photo.
Richard Stevenson Collection

From 1895 to 1902 the company went into the secondhand market to buy thirteen more cars at prices ranging from £60 to £115 per vehicle. Due to widespread electrification the market for horse trams was depressed; most ended up being dismantled or sold as garden sheds.

Livery of the WSELT trams was originally light blue and primrose, but latterly a more serviceable dark maroon was employed with cream window frames and rocker panels.

The first order for Gravesend included four enclosed single deckers and one cross bench or toast rack car. One can only assume the latter was brought out when the sun shone! After complaints about the service from the local council, four single deck cars were replaced by double deckers. Two had knifeboard seating on the top deck; two were fitted with transverse garden type seats. In 1899 two of the remaining single deck vehicles were sold to Lincoln.

All tramcars operating in London had to be licensed annually by the Metropolitan Police. This Metropolitan Stage Carriage (MSC) licence plate was affixed to each vehicle. It was an offence for any unlicensed tramcar to operate on the public highway.

Electric Trams

Electric trams were built to last. The first vehicles were solidly constructed with wooden bodies and metal fittings. Four wheel (single truck) and eight wheel (bogie) trucks were built to withstand the stresses and strains of everyday service. Seating capacity is given for lower saloon (LS) and upper saloon (US). The top deck of many trams was open to the elements initially, but the progressive LCC soon enclosed the upper saloon for the greater convenience of passengers and crews.

Open platforms were the norm. Driver's windscreens were eventually fitted to London trams and were standard throughout the post war LPTB/LTE fleet.

Dimensions are quoted in imperial units. These were customary during the tramway era.

Gravesend & Northfleet

Two four wheel, single deck cars were supplied by the Falcon Engineering Company of Loughborough for the short lived Northfleet experiment. Each vehicle seated 20 people and, it is stated, consumed current at 60 amps with a line voltage of 165. Electricity was fed to the car by means of plough device inserted into a side slot conduit.

The fate of both trams is currently unknown, but it is possible that at least one of these pioneer vehicles was stripped of its motors to be used as an extra to the horsecar fleet.

London County Council

The LCC fleet has been covered at some length in other publications. Service cars equipped solely for conduit operation could only run as far as Woolwich change pit on Market Hill. In practice, trams furnished with trolley poles worked the local routes in the area under review.

Various members of the fleet were renovated in the Pullmanisation programme begun in 1926, which included improvements to seating and interior design of the vehicles.

Livery was originally cream or primrose with 'Preston' style Midland red/ purple lake. This later weathered to a dark brown colour. From 1926 some cars began to appear in experimental liveries. Standard colours of crimson and cream then adorned most of the fleet with the exception of older vehicles of classes A, C and D.

Class A cars 1-100 were delivered in 1903. They only appeared in Woolwich from 1921, after they had received cover top decks and trolley poles.

Class E cars 402-551, 602-751 dated from 1905/6. Cars 402-511 were fitted with trolley poles in the mid 1920s.

Class E/1 cars 752-1426, 1477-1676 dated from 1907/9. Fitted with double trolley poles, cars 1350-1353, 1366-1400 were used on the Eltham route.

Class E/3 cars 1904-2003, 161-210 (II) were introduced in 1930/1. They possessed all metal 74 seat bodies. The main batch were for service on the Kingsway Subway routes, but some were tested in the Woolwich area before transfer to other duties.

Tramcars used on the Woolwich - Abbey Wood route from 1908.

Class B
Cars 102-201. 1903. Electric Railway & Tramway Carriage Works, Preston. Open top, canopied, double deck, reversed stairs. LS22/US34. Brill 21E 6ft 6ins wheelbase trucks. Dick Kerr 25A motors. Dick Kerr DB1-D controllers.

Overall length 28ft 9 ins. Overall width 7ft 1ins. Height over trolley plank 9ft 9½ins.

These vehicles were originally delivered with conduit gear only. Trolley poles were fitted to cars 104, 118, 124, 150, 175, 178, 185 and 196; direct 90° stairs replaced the original reversed variety. These trams were reclassified B/4.

After receiving enclosed top decks a number of these vehicles became surplus to requirements and were sold to other operators including Bexley (qv).

Class D
Cars 302-376, 377-401. 1904. Brush Electrical & Engineering Company, Loughborough (302-376). British Electric Car Company (377-401). Open top, canopied, double deck, reversed stairs. LS28/US38. McGuire maximum traction trucks. 4ft wheelbase, 13ft 6ins total wheelbase. Westinghouse 200 motors. Westinghouse controllers.

Overall length 33ft 6ins. Overall width 7ft 1ins. Height over trolley plank 9ft 9½ins.

Delivered for conduit current collection only. Cars 350, 354, 393 plus one other, 343 or 373, were fitted with direct 90° stairs and trolley poles. They were reclassified D/4.

Tramcars and trailers used on the Woolwich - Eltham, Woolwich - Abbey Wood routes from 1910.

Class M

Cars 1427, 1428-1476, 1677-1726. 1908 (1427) 1910 rest of the class. LCC (1427), Hurst Nelson (1428-1476), Brush (1677-1726). Enclosed top deck, direct 90° stairs. LS24/US38. LCC class 5, swing bolster single truck. 7ft 6ins wheelbase. Westinghouse 220 motors. Westinghouse T2C controllers.

Overall length 29ft 4ins. Overall width 7ft 2ins. Height over trolley plank 15ft 9¾ins.

Individual histories of cars employed in Woolwich/Eltham:

1427 October 1929, Central Repair Depot, Charlton - complete overhaul, Pullmanisation, single trolley fitted. October 1929 Abbey Wood Depot. September 1930 Leyton Depot.

1428-1437 June/July 1910 delivered to Abbey Wood Depot for completion. 1913/14 trailer equipment fitted. 1915 conduit equipment fitted. September/October 1929 CRD overhaul and Pullmanisation, then back to Abbey Wood Depot. September 1930/June 1931 Leyton Depot.

An M class car has been coupled to former horsecar 385 before the whole set leaves the confines of Charlton Works for a trial spin along the Woolwich Road. The Metropolitan Police, as the licensing authority, envisaged problems for trailer car operation in the capital. Nevertheless, the experiment went ahead, using local routes 42 and 44 as a test bed.

1713 Delivered to Abbey Wood Depot for completion 1910. 1913/14 trailer equipment fitted. 1915 conduit equipment fitted. 1921/22 Camberwell Depot. June 1933 CRD complete overhaul, stored Abbey Wood Depot then Bexley Depot for LPTB takeover.

1714-1716, 1718, 1723 Delivered to Abbey Wood Depot for completion 1910. 1913/14 trailer equipment fitted. 1915 conduit equipment fitted. 1921/22 Camberwell Depot.

1717, 1719 Delivered to Abbey Wood for completion 1910. 1913/14 trailer equipment fitted. 1915 conduit equipment fitted. 1921-22 Camberwell Depot. May 1933 CRD complete overhaul, trialled in Bexleyheath and then stored at Abbey Wood Depot. June 1933 stored at Bexley Depot for LPTB takeover.

1721, 1722, 1724-1726 Delivered to Abbey Wood Depot for completion 1910. 1913/14 trailer equipment fitted. 1915 conduit equipment fitted. 1928 Leyton Depot.

Unpowered Trailer Cars

In the Woolwich area a maximum of 19/20 trailers were allocated for routes 44/42. They were withdrawn on 27th January 1919. In May 1924 all remaining trailers were put up for sale. Prices ranged from £4 to £5 each! Some ended up as holiday homes on the South Coast.

T1-T8 Conversions of former North Metropolitan Tramways horsecars. Originally without canopies, they were rebuilt with steel underframes, canopies and new decency panels on the upper deck. They had direct 90° stairs.

T8-T158. 1914. Brush of Loughborough. Open top, canopied, double deck, direct 90° stairs. LS18/US30. Truck wheelbase 6ft 9ins. Overall length 27ft 2ins, overall width 7ft 1ins, height to floor of upper deck 9ft.

Bexley Urban District Council
Bexley UDC Tramways & Dartford Light Railways Joint Committee

Cars 1-12, 13-16. 1903/4. Electric Railway & Tramway Carriage Works, Preston. Open top, canopied, double deck, reversed stairs. LS22/US30. Brush Type A 6ft wheelbase trucks. Dick Kerr 25A motors. Dick Kerr DB1-C controllers.

Overall length 27ft 6ins, overall width 6ft 9ins, height over trolley plank 9ft 9½ins.

These vehicles were later reclassified class A. The original running gear was replaced in 1913 with Peckham Pendulum 8ft wheelbase trucks, except car 9 which received a Brill 21E truck of 6ft wheelbase.

Cars 17-39. Ex LCC B class. These vehicles had enclosed top decks. Their conduit gear was removed before service in Bexley. LS22/US38. Height over trolley plank 16ft 4ins.

Livery was maroon and cream. From 1917 chocolate brown was the predominant colour.

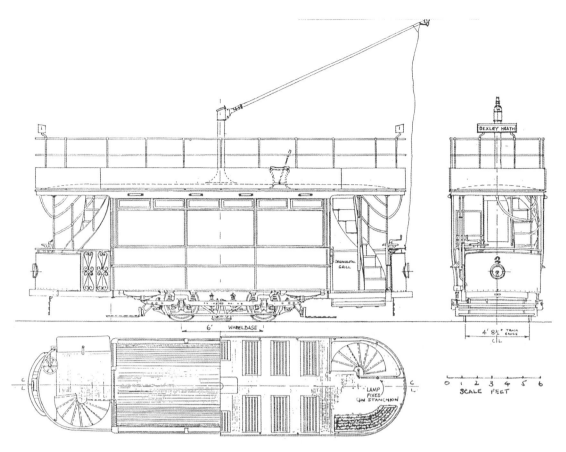

Plan of Dartford car 2, a classic British open top design.

What a splendid sight car 11 must have been when newly placed in service. Pictured on the main line route from Northumberland Heath to Abbey Wood, this apple green and cream liveried vehicle would have turned heads. Note especially the wrought iron work enclosing the upper deck balcony. All in all, this was a fine product of the Brush Works in Loughborough.

Dartford Urban District Council

<u>Cars 1-12</u>. 1906. United Electric Car Company, Preston. Open top, canopied, double deck, direct 180° stairs. LS22/US32. Brill 21E 6ft wheelbase trucks. Dick Kerr motors and controllers.

Overall length 28ft, overall width 7ft, height over trolley plank 9ft 9½ins.

<u>Car 13</u>. Ex Erith Demi Car 15.

All Dartford trams destroyed by fire on 7th August 1917. Livery was maroon and pale yellow.

Erith Urban District Council

<u>Cars 1-6, 9</u>. 1905. Brush of Loughborough. Open top, canopied, double deck, direct 180° stairs. LS22/US30. Mountain & Gibson 21EM 6ft wheelbase trucks. Westinghouse 49B motors. Westinghouse 90M controllers.

Overall length 28ft, overall width 7ft, height over trolley plank 9ft 9½ins.

<u>Cars 7, 8, 10-14</u>. 1906. Brush of Loughborough. Covered top, canopied, open balconies, double deck, direct 180° stairs. LS22/US26. Mountain & Gibson 21EM 6ft wheelbase trucks. Westinghouse 49B motors. Westinghouse 90M controllers.

Overall length 28ft, overall width 7ft, height over trolley plank 16ft 1¾ins.

By the end of the 1920s the Erith fleet appeared rather dowdy and, quite frankly, somewhat antique in appearance. This impression was enhanced by the dark chocolate livery, which looked distinctly unattractive. Car 9 is depicted at the end of the line in Abbey Wood, a location dwarfed nowadays by the flyover carrying the highway to Thamesmead.

Cars 15, 16. 1906. GC Milnes, Voss Company. Single deck demi cars. LS20. Mountain & Gibson special single truck, 5ft 6ins wheelbase. Motors and controllers by Raworth.

Overall length 22ft 6ins, overall width 6ft 8ins, height over trolley plank 10ft 5½ins.

Car 15 sold to Dartford. Car 16 sold to Doncaster.

Cars 15-18 (II). (ex London United Tramways. Type W cars 187, 192, 221, 252). 1902 (acquired 1922). George F Milnes, Birkenhead. Open top, uncanopied, double deck, double flight stairs. LS30/US44. Brill 22E trucks of 4ft wheelbase, total wheelbase 14ft. Westinghouse 49B motors. Westinghouse 90M controllers.

Overall length 34ft 7½ins, overall width 7ft, height over trolley plank 9ft 11½ins.

Canopies added by Erith in 1922, plus direct 180° stairs in place of the original LUT design.

Car 19. (ex Hull Corporation car 101). 1903 (acquired 1916). Hull Corporation works. Covered top, uncanopied, double deck, direct 90° stairs. LS30/US46. Brill 22E trucks of 4ft wheelbase, total wheelbase 14ft. Dick Kerr motors. Westinghouse 90 controllers.

Overall length 33ft 6ins, overall width 7ft, height over trolley plank 16ft 2ins.

Very solidly built vehicle, known to staff as the "Tank". Due to lack of magnetic track brakes, this vehicle was not allowed to work over Bexley metals.

Car 20. 1905. Combined sweeping and water car. Mountain & Gibson truck of 5ft 6ins wheelbase. Westinghouse motors and controllers. Little used in latter years.

Livery was originally a pleasant shade of apple green and primrose. From 1917 a dark brown colour (described officially as a dark mahogany red) replaced the green.

Gravesend & Northfleet

Cars 1-10. 1902. Electric Railway & Tramway Carriage Works, Preston. Open top, canopied, double deck, reversed stairs. LS34/US33. Brill 22E trucks of 4ft wheelbase, total wheelbase 20ft. Dick Kerr 25A motors. Dick Kerr DB1.D controllers.

Overall length 34ft 6ins, overall width 6ft 6ins, height over trolley plank 10ft 1½ins.

Vehicles sold in 1904/6.

Cars 11-20. 1902. ER&TCW. Open top, canopied, double deck, reversed stairs. LS22/US26. Brill 21E trucks of 6ft wheelbase. Walker 25hp motors. Dick Kerr DB1.D controllers.

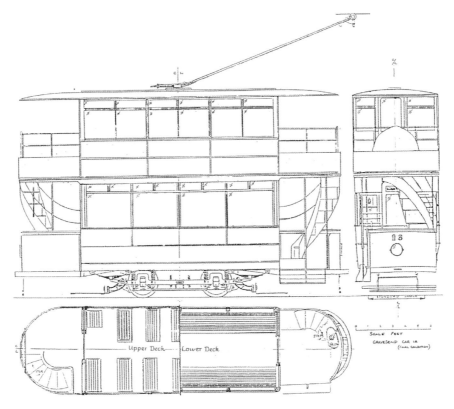

Plan of Gravesend car 18 as rebuilt with a covered top deck.

Pictured outside Denton Post Office, Gravesend car 16 was in many respects a standard ER&TCW product from the works in Preston. The reversed stairs restricted visibility for the motorman. Note the lattice gates to prevent boarding at the driver's end of the tramcar.

Overall length 27ft 4ins, overall width 6ft 6ins, height over trolley plank 9ft 11ins.

Cars 15-20 reconstructed in 1921 with covered tops, manufactured by Beadle, and open balconies. Height over trolley plank 16ft 4ins. There were no railway bridges over roads used by the Gravesend system, hence the above average height for these rebuilds.

Cars 1-4 (II). 1905. Brush of Loughborough. Open top, canopied, double deck, direct 180° stairs. LS22/US26. Brush Aa trucks of 6ft wheelbase. Brush 35hp motors. Brush controllers.

Overall length 28ft, overall width 6ft 6ins, height over trolley plank 9ft 11ins.

Cars 5-6 (II). 1906. Brush of Loughborough. Open top, canopied, double deck, direct 180° stairs. LS20/US23. Brush Aa trucks of 6ft wheelbase. Brush 1002.B motors. Brush HD controllers.

Overall length 26ft 6ins, overall width 6ft 6ins, height over trolley plank 9ft 11ins.

Cars acquired from Jarrow in 1908.

Cars 7, 8 (II). 1905. Brush of Loughborough. Single deck combination cars. LS24. Brush Aa trucks of 6ft wheelbase. Brush 1002.D motors. Brush controllers.

Overall length 25ft 6ins, overall width 6ft 4ins, height over trolley plank 10ft 6ins.

Cars acquired from Taunton in 1921. Their trucks were altered from 3ft 6ins gauge to 4ft 8½ins standard.

Cars 9, 10 (II). 1904. Brush of Loughborough. Single deck demi cars. LS22. Brush special truck of 5ft 6ins wheelbase. Brush 1002.A motors. Raworth Miniature controllers.

Overall length 20ft 11ins, overall width 6ft 3ins, height over trolley plank 10ft 10½ins.

Livery was maroon and cream. Later this was altered to a bright cherry red and ivory.

London Passenger Transport Board
Ex Municipal Cars from 1st July 1933

Bexley class A 1-16. July 1933 Bexley Depot, numbers suffixed by C. September 1933 LT fleet numbers 2066-2081 allocated but never carried. February 1934 all cars withdrawn, stored Brixton Hill Depot. June/August 1934 all cars scrapped at Brixton Hill.

Bexley class B 17-33. July 1933 Bexley Depot, numbers suffixed by C. September 1933 LT fleet numbers 2082-2098 allocated but never carried. September 1933 - May 1934 17C-19C, 21C-26C, 28C-33C withdrawn on replacement by class M cars. Stored at Brixton Hill Depot (some at New Cross Depot en route). October 1933 20C, 27C Abbey Wood Depot. June/ August 1934 all cars scrapped at Brixton Hill.

Erith 1-6, 9, 15-19. July 1933 Erith Depot, numbers suffixed by D. September 1933 LT fleet numbers 2099-2117 allocated but never carried. September 1933 4D, 1D stored at Abbey Wood Depot. 3D, 5D, 15D-19D at Brixton Hill Depot. December 1933 2D at Abbey Wood Depot. January 1934 2D withdrawn, stored at Brixton Hill Depot. July 1934 6D, 9D withdrawn, stored at Abbey Wood Depot. June 1934 6D, 9D stored Brixton Hill Depot.

   June/August 1934 1D, 4D, 18D-19D scrapped at Brixton Hill. September 1934 6D scrapped at Brixton Hill. October 1934 9D scrapped at Brixton Hill. November 1934 3D, 5D scrapped at Brixton Hill. August 1935 2D scrapped at Brixton Hill.

Erith 7, 8, 10-14. July 1933 Erith Depot, numbers suffixed by D. Car 8D MSC licence 640 surrendered, car stored at Erith Depot. Car 13D MSC licence 5269 surrendered, car stored at Erith Depot. September 1933 car 12D MSC licence 5751 surrendered, car stored at Erith Depot. October 1933 car 10D MSC licence 5742 surrendered, car stored at Erith Depot. November 1933 car 8D at CRD for complete overhaul, relicensed MSC 288N. November 1933 car 8D at Erith Depot.

Plan of Erith car 10D in LPTB condition.

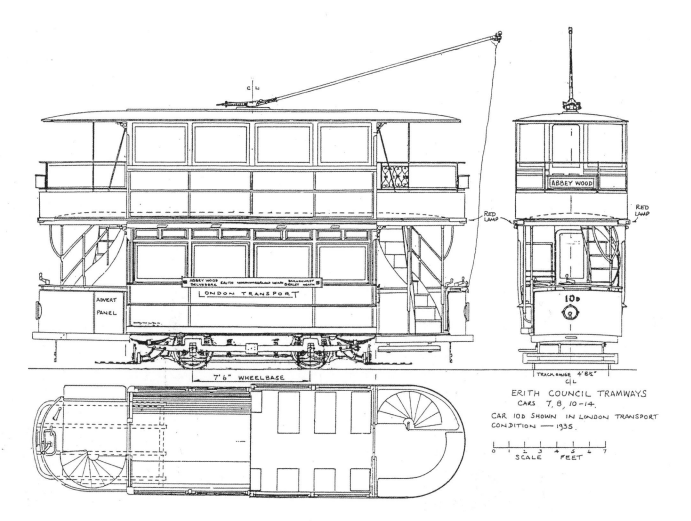

December 1933 car 11D MSC licence 4527 surrendered. Car 10D at CRD for complete overhaul, relicensed MSC 2422N. Cars 7D, 8D, 10D, 11D-14D at Abbey Wood Depot. January/March 1934 all cars through CRD, retrucked on ex Croydon class W/1 trucks and repainted in LPTB livery.

January 1934 car 12D relicensed MSC 1560N, original truck placed under body of ex East Ham car 26. Car 11D relicensed MSC 2194N. February 1934 car 13D relicensed MSC 2861N. January/March 1934 all cars at Abbey Wood Depot. June 1934 car 14D at CRD. Car 14D at Abbey Wood Depot. October 1935 car 10D withdrawn and scrapped at Brixton Hill. November 1935 cars 7D, 8D, 11D-14D withdrawn and stored at Brixton Hill, all cars delicensed. February 1936 cars 7D, 8D, 11D-14D scrapped at Brixton Hill Depot.

As well as the M class vehicles, the management at the LPTB transferred three trams from other areas of London, in order to bolster the service before trolleybus conversion.

Car 53 (ex East Ham car 21). July 1933 East Ham Depot. October 1933 partial overhaul at West Ham Works and repainted in LPTB livery. West Ham Depot. Early 1934 car transferred to Abbey Wood Depot. November 1934 complete overhaul at CRD. Abbey Wood Depot. February 1935 MSC licence 5552 surrendered and car withdrawn at Abbey Wood Depot. August 1935 car scrapped at Abbey Wood Depot.

Car 58 (ex East Ham car 11). July 1933 East Ham Depot. August 1933 Car overhauled at West Ham Works and repainted in LPTB livery. West Ham Depot. Early 1934 car transferred to Abbey Wood Depot. September 1934 MSC licence 5568 surrendered and car withdrawn, stored at Abbey Wood. Car scrapped at Abbey Wood Depot.

Car 349 (ex Croydon class W/1 cars 5E, 17E). July 1933 Thornton Heath Depot. December 1933 cars withdrawn and stored at Brixton Hill. 1934 at the CRD the body of car 17E was mounted on the truck of 5E, car was overhauled, magnetic brakes fitted, repainted in LPTB livery, renumbered car 349, seating capacity LS18 (2+1 cushioned seating) US32. Abbey Wood Depot. March 1935 MSC licence 6867 surrendered, car withdrawn and stored at Brixton Hill. October 1935 car scrapped at Brixton Hill.

LCC class M

1468. July 1933 car at Holloway Depot (services 13, 17). November 1933 CRD complete overhaul and trolley fitted. December 1933 Bexley Depot. November 1934 CRD partial overhaul. December 1934 Bexley Depot. November/December 1935 CRD complete overhaul. December 1935 West Ham Depot. June 1937 car scrapped at Walthamstow Depot.

1677. July 1933 car stored unlicensed at Chiswick Depot. September 1933 CRD complete overhaul and relicensed MSC 8670. Erith Depot. December 1933 Abbey Wood Depot. July 1934 Bexley Depot. August 1934 CRD partial

overhaul. September 1935 CRD complete overhaul. Bexley Depot. November 1935 West Ham Depot. August 1937 car scrapped at Walthamstow Depot.
Notes: Single trolley pole. Cleats on dash. Pigtail on cant rail below indicator.

1678. July 1933 car stored unlicensed at Chiswick Depot. October 1933 CRD complete overhaul, K-Ray indicators fitted, relicensed MSC 2608N. October 1933 Bexley Depot. November 1934 CRD partial overhaul. Abbey Wood Depot. October/November 1935 CRD complete overhaul. November 1935 West Ham Depot. October 1937 car scrapped at Walthamstow Depot.

1679. July 1933 car stored unlicensed at Chiswick Depot. August 1933 CRD complete overhaul and relicensed MSC 7821. Bexley Depot. August 1934 CRD partial overhaul. Bexley Depot. August 1935 CRD complete overhaul. November 1935 West Ham Depot. June 1937 car scrapped at Walthamstow Depot.
Notes: Single trolley pole. Cleats on dash. Pigtail on cant rail centre of indicator, but two in panel above indicator one end for pigtail mount, but no sign of holes at other end.

1680. July 1933 car stored unlicensed at Chiswick Depot. October 1933 CRD complete overhaul, relicensed MSC 2606N. Bexley Depot. October 1934 CRD partial overhaul. Bexley Depot. October/November 1935 CRD complete overhaul. November 1935 West Ham Depot. June 1937 car scrapped at Walthamstow Depot.
Notes: Single trolley pole. Cleats on dash. Pigtail on cant rail centre of indicator.

1681. July 1933 car stored unlicensed at Chiswick Depot. September 1933 CRD complete overhaul and relicensed MSC 8442. Erith Depot. December 1933 Abbey Wood Depot. February 1934 CRD partial overhaul. Abbey Wood Depot. June 1934 Bexley Depot. February/March 1935 CRD complete overhaul. November 1935 West Ham Depot. September 1937 car scrapped at Walthamstow Depot.
Notes: K-Ray indicators.

1682. July 1933 Bexley Depot. March 1934 Hampstead Depot. June 1934 car scrapped at Hampstead Depot.

1683. July 1933 car stored unlicensed at Chiswick Depot. September 1933 CRD complete overhaul and relicensed MSC 8811. Erith Depot. December 1933 Abbey Wood Depot. February 1934 CRD partial overhaul. Abbey Wood Depot. March 1935 CRD complete overhaul. Abbey Wood Depot. November 1935 West Ham Depot. May 1937 car scrapped at Walthamstow Depot.
Notes: No cleats. Pigtail on centre panel. Indicator with disc spaces for three code lamps (TCL).

1684. July 1933 car stored unlicensed at Chiswick Depot. November 1933 CRD complete overhaul and relicensed MSC 2610N. Bexley Depot. October

1934 CRD partial overhaul. November 1934 Abbey Wood Depot. October/ November 1935 CRD complete overhaul. November 1935 West Ham Depot. August 1937 car scrapped at Walthamstow Depot.
Notes: K-Ray indicators fitted. Pigtail centre of cant rail below indicator.

1685. July 1933 Bexley Depot. November 1933 CRD complete overhaul. Bexley Depot. November 1934 CRD partial overhaul. Abbey Wood Depot. November 1935 West Ham Depot. August 1937 car scrapped at Walthamstow Depot.

1686. July 1933 Bexley Depot. December 1933 delicensed. March 1934 Hampstead Depot. June 1934 car scrapped at Hampstead Depot.

1687. July 1933 Bexley Depot. February 1934 CRD complete overhaul. Abbey Wood Depot. January 1935 CRD partial overhaul. November 1935 West Ham Depot. August 1937 car scrapped at Walthamstow Depot.

1688. July 1933 car stored unlicensed at Chiswick Depot. October 1933 CRD complete overhaul and relicensed MSC 64N. Erith Depot. December 1933 Abbey Wood Depot. January 1934 Bexley Depot. September 1934 CRD partial overhaul. Bexley Depot. September 1935 CRD complete overhaul. November 1935 West Ham Depot. June 1937 car scrapped at Walthamstow Depot.
Notes: No side opening ventilator windows. Cleats on dash. Pigtails on cant rail centred under indicators.

1689. July 1933 Bexley Depot. May 1934 CRD Partial overhaul. Bexley Depot. February 1935 CRD complete overhaul. Bexley Depot. November 1935 West Ham Depot. August 1937 car scrapped at Walthamstow Depot.
Notes: TCL indicator.

1690. July 1933 Camberwell Depot. November 1933 CRD partial overhaul. Erith Depot. December 1933 Abbey Wood Depot. August 1934 Bexley Depot. December 1934 CRD complete overhaul. Bexley Depot. March 1935 Abbey Wood Depot.

1691. July 1933 Bexley Depot. May 1934 CRD partial overhaul. Bexley Depot. February/March 1935 CRD complete overhaul. Bexley Depot. November 1935 West Ham Depot. March 1938 car scrapped at Walthamstow Depot.
Notes: TCL indicator.

1692. July 1933 car stored unlicensed at Chiswick Depot. CRD complete overhaul and relicensed MSC828N. Erith Depot. December 1933 Abbey Wood Depot. July 1934 CRD partial overhaul. Abbey Wood Depot. July/August 1935 CRD complete overhaul. Abbey Wood Depot. November 1935 West Ham Depot. July 1937 car scrapped at Walthamstow Depot.
Notes: Single trolley pole fitted. Pigtail on cant rail centred under indicator.

1693. July 1933 car stored unlicensed at Chiswick Depot. September 1933 CRD complete overhaul and relicensed MSC47N. Erith Depot. December

1933 Abbey Wood Depot. September 1934 CRD partial overhaul. Abbey Wood Depot. September 1935 CRD complete overhaul. Bexley Depot. November 1935 West Ham Depot. July 1937 car scrapped at Walthamstow Depot.

1694. July 1933 car stored unlicensed at Chiswick Depot. August 1933 CRD complete overhaul and relicensed MSC6847. Bexley Depot. August 1934 CRD partial overhaul. Bexley Depot. July 1935 CRD complete overhaul. Bexley Depot. November 1935 West Ham Depot. July 1937 car scrapped at Walthamstow Depot.
Notes: Single trolley pole fitted. No cleats. Pigtail placed centrally in panel above indicators. K-Ray indicators fitted.

1695. July 1933 car stored unlicensed at Chiswick Depot. October 1933 CRD complete overhaul and relicensed MSC158N. Bexley Depot. October 1934 CRD partial overhaul. Bexley Depot. September/October 1935 CRD complete overhaul. Bexley Depot. November 1935 West Ham Depot. February 1937 car scrapped at Walthamstow Depot.

1696. July 1933 car stored unlicensed at Chiswick Depot. September 1933 CRD complete overhaul and relicensed MSC4213. Bexley Depot. September 1934 CRD partial overhaul. Bexley Depot. August/September 1935 CRD complete overhaul. Bexley Depot. November 1935 West Ham Depot. August 1937 car scrapped at Walthamstow Depot.
Notes: Pigtail on cant rail centred above indicator.

1697. July 1933 Leyton Depot. October 1933 CRD complete overhaul. Bexley Depot. October 1934 CRD partial overhaul. November 1934 Bexley Depot. October/November 1935 CRD complete overhaul. Bexley Depot. November 1935 West Ham Depot. October 1937 car scrapped at Walthamstow Depot.
Notes: Pigtail on cant rail centred under indicator. Plain indicator one end, K-Ray indicator at other.

1698. July 1933 Camberwell Depot. October 1933 CRD partial overhaul. Erith Depot. December 1933 Abbey Wood Depot. October 1934 CRD complete overhaul. Abbey Wood Depot. November 1935 West Ham Depot. December 1937 car scrapped at Walthamstow Depot.
Notes: Single trolley pole fitted.

1699. July 1933 car stored unlicensed at Chiswick Depot. CRD complete overhaul, K-Ray indicators fitted and relicensed MSC5269. Bexley Depot. July 1934 CRD partial overhaul. Bexley Depot. July/August 1935 CRD complete overhaul. Bexley Depot. November 1935 West Ham Depot. July 1937 car scrapped at Walthamstow Depot.

1700. July 1933 Bexley Depot. September 1933 Erith Depot. December 1933 Abbey Wood Depot. May 1934 CRD partial overhaul. Bexley Depot. March 1935 CRD complete overhaul. Bexley Depot. November 1935 West Ham Depot. October 1937 car scrapped at Walthamstow Depot.

Notes: Single trolley pole fitted. Pigtail on cant rail centred under indicator. TCL indicators.

1701. July 1933 car stored unlicensed at Chiswick Depot. August 1933 CRD complete overhaul and relicensed MSC2520N. Bexley Depot. May 1934 CRD partial overhaul. Bexley Depot. April 1935 CRD completc overhaul. Bexley Depot. November 1935 West Ham Depot. June 1937 car scrapped at Walthamstow Depot.
Notes: Single trolley pole fitted.

1702. July 1933 car stored unlicensed at Chiswick Depot. November 1933 CRD complete overhaul and relicensed MSC2609N. Bexley Depot. October 1934 CRD partial overhaul. November 1934 Bexley Depot. October 1935 CRD complete overhaul. Bexley Depot. November 1935 West Ham Depot. October 1937 car scrapped at Walthamstow Depot.
Notes: Single trolley pole fitted.

1703. July 1933 Bexley Depot. January 1934 Brixton Hill Depot. June 1934 car scrapped at Brixton Hill Depot.

1704. July 1933 car stored unlicensed at Chiswick Depot. October 1933 CRD complete overhaul and relicensed MSC2605N. Bexley Depot. October 1934 CRD partial overhaul. Bexley Depot. October 1935 CRD complete overhaul. Bexley Depot. November 1935 West Ham Depot. December 1937 car scrapped at Walthamstow Depot.

M class car 1705 stands on Bexley Depot forecourt. It has been repainted in LPTB red livery but lacks the LONDON TRANSPORT lettering on the waist panel. These trams were sturdily constructed and rode on 'unusual' swing bolster single trucks, which gave a memorable fore, aft and sideways ride for passengers, quite unlike that normally experienced on a conventional Brill 21E truck.
London Transport Museum

Erith Council followed the lead of Gravesend and ordered two demi cars to breathe life into the Northend route. As far as we know, no pictures of these elusive vehicles have ever surfaced. Richard Elliott of the TLRS partly remedied the situation by constructing this 1:16 scale model. Note the pleasant green and cream livery. When your author interviewed Richard and former tram driver George Tapp, opinions were divided as to the style of trolley base used by the prototype. At one stage an open top trolley standard was used, so that the trolley pole on the single decker did not foul double deck specials as they passed one another at peak times on the Northend line.

Advertisements on tramcars added a splash of colour to the street scene. Unfortunately, in an era of monochromatic photography this feature is often lost to posterity. Expert model maker, Richard Elliott, knew the Bexley system in his youth and was therefore able to produce this accurate scale replica of car 9. The green Maples poster frequently appeared on public transport in London. *Richard Elliott/TLRS Archive*

Apprentice coach makers were sometimes set a task to reproduce their full size work in miniature. These models are scarce, but give us a good insight into liveries and vehicle design of the period. Woolwich horsecar 4 has been restored to around 1890s condition; it retains back to back knifeboard seating on the top deck. Note the different colour woods used in the construction.

Unlike restored car 106, the vast majority of early electric tramcars were sacrificed to the scrap heap, before the preservation movement got going. Reappearance in model form helps to give an impression of the lost prototype. Frank Wilson, one time chairman of the Tramway and Light Railway Society, constructed this 1:16 scale version of car 1435. It is depicted on Eltham route 44 and has fittings on the dash for trailer car operation. Frank knew these vehicles and recreated one accurately in miniature. *John Prentice/TLRS Archive*

1705. July 1933 car stored unlicensed at Chiswick Depot. August 1933 CRD complete overhaul and relicensed MSC2596. Bexley Depot. August 1934 CRD partial overhaul. Bexley Depot. August 1935 CRD complete overhaul. November 1935 West Ham Depot. August 1937 car scrapped at Walthamstow Depot.

1706. July 1933 car stored unlicensed at Chiswick Depot. July 1933 CRD complete overhaul and relicensed MSC2521N. Bexley Depot. June 1934 CRD partial overhaul. Bexley Depot. May 1935 CRD complete overhaul. Bexley Depot. November 1935 West Ham Depot. July 1937 car scrapped at Walthamstow Depot.

1707. July 1933 car stored unlicensed at Chiswick Depot. CRD complete Overhaul and relicensed MSC388N. Bexley Depot. July 1934 CRD partial overhaul. Bexley Depot. July 1935 CRD complete overhaul. July 1937 car scrapped at Walthamstow Depot.
Notes: TCL indicator.

1708. July 1933 car stored unlicensed at Chiswick Depot. CRD complete overhaul and relicensed MSC2522N. Erith Depot. December 1933 Abbey Wood Depot. June 1934 CRD partial overhaul. Abbey Wood Depot. May 1935 CRD complete overhaul. Abbey Wood Depot. November 1935 West Ham Depot. June 1937 car scrapped at Walthamstow Depot.

1709. July 1933 car stored unlicensed at Chiswick Depot. October 1933 CRD complete overhaul and relicensed MSC2569N. Bexley Depot. October 1934 CRD partial overhaul. Bexley Depot. September/October 1935 CRD complete overhaul. Bexley Depot. November 1935 West Ham Depot. August 1937 car scrapped at Walthamstow Depot.

1710. July 1933 Camberwell Depot. August 1933 Bexley Depot or Abbey Wood Depot (conflicting information sources). March 1934 CRD partial overhaul. November 1935 West Ham Depot. June 1937 car scrapped at Walthamstow Depot.
Notes: Pigtail on cant rail centred under indicator. TCL indicators.

1711. July 1933 car stored unlicensed at Chiswick Depot. CRD complete overhaul and relicensed MSC2523N. Bexley Depot. May 1934 CRD partial overhaul, number stencils fitted. Bexley Depot. April/May 1935 CRD complete overhaul. Bexley Depot. November 1935 West Ham Depot. September 1937 car scrapped at Walthamstow Depot.
Notes: No cleats. Pigtail on cant rail centred under indicator. Plain panel indicators.

1712. July 1933 Bexley Depot. Unknown date, stored at New Cross Depot, then Brixton Hill. June 1934 car scrapped at Brixton Hill Depot.

1713. July 1933 Bexley Depot. March 1934 Hampstead Depot. June 1934 car scrapped at Hampstead Depot.

1714. July 1933 car stored unlicensed at Chiswick Depot. CRD complete overhaul and relicensed MSC28N. Bexley Depot. June 1934 CRD partial overhaul. Bexley Depot. June 1935 CRD complete overhaul. Bexley Depot. November 1935 West Ham Depot. June 1937 car scrapped at Walthamstow Depot.

1717. July 1933 Bexley Depot. July 1934 CRD partial overhaul. June/July 1935 CRD complete overhaul. Bexley Depot. November 1935 West Ham Depot. August 1937 car scrapped at Walthamstow Depot.
Notes: Cleats on dash. Pigtail on cant rail centred under indicator. TCL indicator.

1718. July 1933 Leyton Depot. Bexley Depot. January 1934 CRD partial overhaul. Bexley Depot. January/February 1935 CRD complete overhaul. November 1935 West Ham Depot. October 1936 car scrapped at Walthamstow Depot.
Notes: Two trolley poles fitted. No number stencil holders.

1719. July 1933 Bexley Depot. CRD partial overhaul. June/July 1935 CRD complete overhaul. November 1935 West Ham Depot. July 1937 car scrapped at Walthamstow Depot.
Notes: Single trolley pole fitted. Pigtail on cant rail centred under indicator.

1720. July 1933 Leyton Depot. August 1933 Bexley Depot. November 1933 CRD complete overhaul. Bexley Depot. November 1934 CRD partial overhaul. Bexley Depot. November/December 1935 CRD complete overhaul. West Ham Depot. June 1937 car scrapped at Walthamstow Depot.

1722. July 1933 Leyton Depot. March 1934 West Ham Works partial overhaul. Leyton Depot. July 1934 Abbey Wood Depot. March 1935 CRD complete overhaul. Abbey Wood Depot. November 1935 Delicensed. CRD staff car based at New Cross Depot. March 1937 car scrapped at Croydon Depot.
Notes: Two trolley poles fitted. TCL indicators.

1724. July 1933 Leyton Depot. November 1933 CRD or West Ham Works, partial overhaul, double trolleys replaced by a single pole. Leyton or Bexley Depot. May 1934 Abbey Wood Depot. December 1934 CRD complete overhaul. Abbey Wood Depot. November 1935 West Ham Depot. June 1937 car scrapped at Walthamstow Depot.
Notes: Pigtail lower than usual, but above indicator.

1725. July 1933 CRD complete overhaul and relicensed MSC15N. Bexley Depot. May 1934 Abbey Wood Depot. June 1934 CRD partial overhaul. Bexley Depot. June 1935 CRD complete overhaul. Bexley Depot. November 1935 West Ham Depot. July 1937 car scrapped at Walthamstow Depot.
Notes: Single trolley pole fitted. Cleats on dash. Pigtail on cant rail centred under indicator. K-Ray indicators fitted.

Trolleybuses

As at the beginning of 1945 the following trolleybuses were attached to Bexleyheath Depot. A total of 78 vehicles were recorded. The depot was later classified BX by London Transport. Class is followed by fleet number.

B2 104

C3 305, 306, 327, 329, 330

D2 388, 393, 399, 400, 410, 411, 413, 414, 423-427, 429, 434, 438-442, 444, 465, 469, 471-473.

D3 539

E1 593, 595

E2 608, 609

E3 637

H1 765, 785, 796, 798, 800, 802, 805, 807, 810, 811, 813, 850, 889, 890, 893

J2 969, 971-974

K1 1063, 1066, 1097

K2 1321

L3 1406, 1407, 1527, 1528

M1 1546-1549

N1 1585

P1 1699, 1702-1704, 1711, 1712, 1720

As at August 1951 a total of 83 trolleybuses were stationed locally; the vehicle fleet numbers at BX Depot were as follows:

94, 96, 97C, 98C, 104, 106, 385C, 388, 389C, 390B, 391B, 392B, 393, 395B, 396C, 397C, 399, 400, 401, 402C, 403, 404, 405B, 407B, 408, 409B, 410, 412B, 414, 415C, 419C, 416, 417, 423, 424, 426, 427, 429-432, 439-442, 444, 451B, 468, 469, 470B, 471-476, 480, 483, 765, 784B, 785, 786B, 788, 789, 790B, 793, 794B, 796-798, 799B, 800, 802, 801B, 805-807, 808B, 809-811, 813, 850

The B suffix indicates vehicles rebodied by East Lancashire Coachbuilders of Blackburn after war damage. Suffix C applies to trolleybuses reconstructed by Northern Coachbuilders of Newcastle-upon-Tyne. The Bexley routes were well known for providing a home for these rebuilds.

Scrapping of most of the local trolleybuses took place at Penhall Road, Charlton in 1959. Newsreels featuring this unedifying process can be viewed on the internet.

D2 class 395B (DGY 395) was one of the vehicles rebodied after war damage. It is depicted here on the county boundary at Knee Hill, Abbey Wood. This location was well known for its plethora of overhead wires including a trolleybus turning circle. The Bexley system often featured short workings, but in this case 395B is heading for Parson's Hill, Woolwich.
LCCTT Roy Hubble